For my wife and son

Contents

Preface..vii

Chapter 1   The History of Driving Under the Influence.....1

Chapter 2   The DUI Stop and Arrest 25

Chapter 3   Breath/Blood Testing 51

Chapter 4   DUI Court Procedures....................................67

Chapter 5   DUI Penalties & Conditions 77

Chapter 6   Alcohol/Drug Evaluations, Classes, and
            Treatment..91

Chapter 7   Department of Licensing/Motor Vehicles.....115

Chapter 8   DUI Defenses And Avoiding
            A (Another) DUI...131

Chapter 9   The Court, Prosecutor, Judge, and Plea
            Negotiations 157

Chapter 10 Alcohol, Drugs and the Human Body 167

Chapter 11 Choosing an Attorney 197

Chapter 12 Miscellaneous DUI Issues 205

Chapter 13 Washington State Statutes/Case Law.............219

Chapter 14 Definitions..247

Preface

This is the second edition of *"The DUI Handbook for the Accused"* and follows the same general format used in the first edition of the book. Namely, the book is directed specifically at those individuals who have been charged with the crime of driving under the influence (DUI) of alcohol and/or drugs. However, this book has used the previous format as a foundation and has been expanded to provide more real world information and material. Further, it has been four years since the first edition was published and hence, the second edition has also updated some of the information in the previous edition.

The first edition of this book was unique as it was the first book in the United States designed to help and inform the person charged with DUI through an extraordinarily intense, stressful, and complicated time. The book detailed every component of the DUI process in a way that had never previously been attempted. However, despite the novelty of the book and the details provided there was room to improve.

This new edition of the *"The DUI Handbook for the Accused,"* still provides the reader information on DUI laws, the DUI process, DUI court procedures, how to choose an attorney, information on the court, prosecuting attorney and plea negotiation, options for the DUI defendant, DUI defenses, DUI Penalties, Driving of Licensing issues, alcohol/drugs and the human body, and the many other collateral consequences of driving under the influence. However, the new edition adds a chapter on the history of DUI, more than 360 legal issues and defenses to DUI (the first edition documented 60 legal issues and defenses) and a new section that details the alcohol/drug evaluation and diagnosis process (the goal is to get the most realistic and honest alcohol evaluation but also to provide help to those people who need help with their addiction).

If you have been charged with a DUI, please read this book thoroughly and seek advice from an experienced, reputable, and DUI focused attorney. Their advice is invaluable and no book can replace competent representation. Ultimately the goal of any attorney in the DUI realm is to protect you and your valuable rights, fight hard for the best result possible and, speaking personally, do everything to ensure that you do not find yourself in this difficult position again. Good luck.

CHAPTER 1

The History of Driving Under the Influence

The combination of consuming alcohol and operating modes of transportation has occurred for thousands of years. The use of animals as transportation was most certainly done under the influence too many times to chronicle. It was probably unwise and led to many a disaster but prior to modern times it was never illegal. Moreover, this type of activity rarely endangered anybody or anything other than the operator and the animal.

In more modern times the Industrial Revolution introduced the world to motorized transportation, namely locomotives and the great railroad movement. This is really genesis in regards to operating a motorized form of transportation under the influence of alcohol. Locomotives traveled at great speed carrying many passengers and there was real danger of serious tragedy if something went wrong. This issue became more severe if the train engineer was operating while under the influence of alcohol. To that end, in the United States in 1843 the New York Central Railroad prohibited drinking by employees while on duty. Borkenstein, Robert F. *Historical Perspective: North American Traditional and Experimental Response.* Journal of Studies on Alcohol, suppl. 10:3-12 (1985) In 1904 the *Quarterly Journal of Inebriety* editorialized, with a hint of things to come, that "the precaution of railroad companies to have only total abstainers guide their engines will soon extend to the owners of these new motor wagons. . . .With the increased popularity of these wagons, accidents of this kind will multiply rapidly." Crothers, T.D. M.D, Editor. *Quarterly Journal of Inebriety.* Hartford, MA. (1904) However, such conduct as operating a vehicle while under the influence of alcohol was not yet a crime.

The first law directly related to drinking and "driving" was enacted in 1872 and it was not for another twenty-four years that England saw its first drunk driving fatality. This is largely due to the fact that there were very few modes of motorized transport, few roads capable of serving such a machine, and that the automobile as we know it was not even invented until 1885. However, the day would invariably come when a tragic event involving an automobile would occur.

In 1869 well known Irish scientist Mary Ward became the first automobile accident fatality. During this period the development of steam powered vehicles was all the rage and one such vehicle was developed by William Parsons and his sons. In 1869 Mary and her husband were traveling in the Parsons vehicle in Ireland with the Parsons boys and their tutor when Mary was thrown from the vehicle while it was rounding a bend in the road. Mary fell under the steel wheel and apparently died almost instantly. A doctor lived near the scene of the accident and arrived shortly after the accident occurred and found Mary cut, bruised and bleeding from the ears. She died from a broken neck. *Profile of Mary Ward.* Irish

Universities Promoting Science Group.

Twenty seven years later the world's second known traffic fatality involving the automobile occurred. On August 17, 1896, 44 year old Bridget Driscoll was killed while crossing the grounds of the Crystal Palace in Hyde Park, London. Bridget was with her daughter May, and was struck by an automobile owned by the Anglo-French Motor Carriage Company. The company was displaying its new creation and it was being used to give demonstration rides. Witnesses proclaimed the vehicle was traveling at a "reckless pace, in fact, like a fire engine," but the driver, Arthur James Edsall claimed to be travelling at only 4 mile per hour. *History of Road Safety.* Cardiff Council Road Safety Centre. http://www.roadsafety. cardiff.gov.uk/history. Controversially, Mr. Edsall's passenger Alice Standing claimed that the engine was modified to allow the vehicle to travel faster and possibly reach speeds as fast as 4.5 mile per hour! The matter proceeded to the civil courts and eventually to trial where the jury returned a verdict of "accidental death." The coroner, Percy Morrison said he hoped "such a thing would never happen again." Mr. Edsall was not criminally prosecuted. *Id.*

It was not long after Mrs. Driscoll's life was tragically cut short by the automobile when the world experienced the very first arrest for driving under the influence. Like Mrs. Driscoll's happening, the first DUI arrest occurred in London, England. On September 10, 1897, London Taxi cab driver George Smith (age 25) was arrested for driving under the influence when the taxi he was driving drove onto the pavement and collided with the building located at 165 Bond Street, London. Mr. Smith, who worked for the Electric Cab Company of Hackney, London, allegedly admitted to "having had two or three glasses of beer." He was later convicted and fined 20 shillings (no jail). www.history.com

The taxi cab company that employed Mr. Smith shortly thereafter was involved in a far more tragic event. Thirteen days after Mr. Smith's historic arrest, Stephen Kempton, aged 9, was crushed to death when the coat he was wearing got caught in the chain drive of the electric taxi after he had jumped onto the outside of a cab. The Electric Cab Company ceased trading in August, 1899 with all of its 77 vehicles being sold. A year later, the London Metropolitan Police stopped licensing this type of electric cab. http://www.encyclo.co.uk/calendar/September.php The first known traffic fatality (non-alcohol related) in the United States occurred on September 10, 1899, in New York City. Henry Hale Bliss was disembarking a streetcar at West 74th Street and Central Park West when an electric-powered taxicab (Automobile Number 43) collided with him crushing his head and chest. *Fatally Hurt by Automobile*. New York Times article. (September 14, 1899) Henry died the next morning from his injuries. The driver of the taxi, Arthur Smith, was arrested and charged with manslaughter. He was later acquitted based on the defense that the conduct that resulted in Mr. Bliss' death was unintentional. Interestingly, the passenger in the taxicab was Dr. David Edson, the son of former New York City mayor Franklin Edson. The location of this accident is memorialized with a plague that reads:

> Here at West 74th Street and Central Park West, Henry H. Bliss dismounted from a streetcar and was struck and knocked unconscious by an automobile on the evening of September 13, 1899. When Mr. Bliss, a New York real estate man, died the next morning from his injuries, he became the first recorded motor

vehicle fatality in the Western Hemisphere. This sign was erected to remember Mr. Bliss on the centennial of his untimely death and to promote safety on our streets and highways. *Id.*

Prior to any laws in the United States making driving under the influence a crime, another great tragedy occurred involving drunk) driving. In 1907 near Colorado City, Colorado, an accident occurred that killed the four passengers in the car driven by Albert Marksheffel, who survived the accident. Allegedly the accident occurred after the five friends had been drinking at a local Elks Club. After leaving the club Albert lost control of his speeding vehicle, hit some nearby railroad tracks and ended up in the ditch. Laden, Rich. *Sign of old Times / Colorado Springs history posted on streets all.* The Colorado Springs Gazette. (July 17, 2001) This particular case was the cause for many states considering enacting driving under the influence laws. The story of Albert Marksheffel doesn't end with this horrific vehicle accident. The same year, 1907, Albert moved to Colorado Springs and managed the Western Automobile & Supply Company. The year following this DUI accident he opened his own automobile dealership, the Marksheffel Motor Company, and sold Chalmers, Dodge, Cadillac and Chevrolet cars. *Id.* He later co-founded the Colorado Springs Rotary Club and had, rather ironically, a local street named after him, Marksheffel Road. Id.; www.coloradospringsrotary.org

Although Great Britain enacted the first known law making "drinking and driving" illegal in 1872, the United States would not make this activity unlawful for another 38 years. However, prior to this enactment in the United States drinking and driving was in the news. The first reported news article regarding drinking and driving in the United States appeared in 1904 and the following years such activity appeared in newspapers and periodicals more frequently. Even still it was not until 1910 that New York became the first state to enact drinking and driving laws. To give some perspective, the Model T Ford was introduced in 1908 and by the time the first driving under the influence law was introduced, nearly 12,000 of Ford's Model T had been sold. Interestingly, Henry Ford did have an opinion about drinking and driving and his opinion was clear, to wit: "booze had to go when modern industry and the motor came in." Lender, Mark E., and Martin, James K. *Drinking in America: A History*. New York: Free Press (1982)

Following the enactment of New York State's driving under the influence law was enacted other states quickly followed, including California in 1911. Once the law put in place a system whereby a driver could be prosecuted for drunk driving there needed to be a way to measure the driver's level of intoxication. And thus the race was on to invent a machine to accomplish this task. Naturally, prior to the invention of such a machine there was no presumptive level of impairment because there was no way to validate such a level. http://www. borkensteincourse.org

The study of human breath is not a 20th century phenomenon. As far back as 1774 French chemist Antoine Lavoisier conducted studies regarding respiration, but his contribution to the field of breath testing involves his invention, the "gasometer." This invention was the first instrument to make relatively accurate measurements of respiration gases.

In 1803 William Henry formulated a chemical equation that was later known as "Henry's Law" and has had significant impact on the measurement of human breath. Jones,

A.W. *Physiological Aspects of Breath Alcohol Measurement, Alcohol, Drugs and Driving.* 6(2):1-24, Page 12 (1990) Following Henry's impact and more than fifty years after Lavoisier's gasometer design, British and Australian physician John Hutchinson adapted the design and invented the first "spirometer," which was used for measuring the volume of a patient's breath. *The Spirometer, the Stethoscope and the Scale Balance.* London: John Churchill (1852)

In 1874, British physician Francis Anstie went one further and actually trapped human breath and applied colorimetric analysis to study alcohol in the body. Anstie, FE: *Final experiments on the elimination of alcohol from the body.* Practitioner 13:15 (1874)

In 1927 Dr. Emil Bogen reported measuring blood alcohol concentration (BAC) by analyzing a person's breath. Bogen, Emil. *Drunkenness, a quantitative study of acute alcoholic intoxication.* (1927) And, the breath testing device was nearly reality.

Also in 1927, Dr. Gorsky a police surgeon in Britain testified at an early "DUI" trial regarding the "drunkenness" of the defendant. Mitchell, C. Ainsworth. *Science and the Detective.* The American Journal of Police Science (Northwestern University) 3 (2): 169–182 (March/April 1932) The defendant was convicted largely based on the evidence provided by Dr. Gorsky. *Id.*

The first "practical" breath testing machine was invented by Professor Rolla N. Harger in 1938. Called the "Drunk-o-meter" it was intended to be used by police and thereafter as evidence in courts of law. Holcomb, R.L. *Alcohol in Relation to Traffic Accidents.* JAMA, 1076-1085 (1938) Also in 1938 The National Safety Council's Committee on Alcohol and Other Drugs (COAD) (formally known as the Committee on

Tests for Intoxication) collaborated with the American Medical Association's Committee to Study Problems of Motor Vehicle Accidents to establish standards for defining the phrase "under the influence." COAD based these standards, in large part, on Holcomb's research.

In 1939, a year after Harger's "Drunk-o-meter" invention became reality, his home state of Indiana became the first state in America to establish a presumptive alcohol impairment level of 0.15%. The enactment of "presumptive levels" shifted the focus in DUI investigations and trials from simply using officer observations to more "scientific" chemical testing.

The 1940s saw more development of the breath test machinery, with both the "Intoximeter" and "Alcometer" introduced in 1941. In 1944 the National Committee on Uniform Traffic Laws and Ordinances incorporated presumptive alcohol concentrations in the Chemical Tests Section of the Uniform Vehicle Code. In 1948, the CAOD collaborated with "Licensed Beverage Industries, Inc.," to fund a research project at Michigan State College to study breathtesting methods. This study examined the three most prevalent breath-alcohol testing instruments of the time, the Drunkometer, Intoximeter and Alcometer. Each of these instruments utilized wet chemical methods that analyzed breath samples based on chemical interactions between the alcohol molecules and a reagent. The study, effectively the first of its kind, determined that the three instruments could achieve results that were in "close agreement" with direct blood alcohol results. At the time these findings were perceived very favorably by the law enforcement community Immediately following World War II, the National Committee on Uniform Traffic Laws and Ordinances held the first national highway safety conference. http://www.

ncutlo.org/ The government had become concerned with the dramatic increase in highway accidents involving injuries and deaths, due in large part to the higher number of vehicles on the road following World War II. An outcrop of the conference and subsequent studies was a recommendation setting a standard level for blood alcohol impairment at 0.15 %. This number would then become a "target" that states would aspire to in determining when a driver was presumptably impaired. This particular BAC level was also recommended by the American Medical Association (AMA) as an "accepted" level for impairment based on the AMA's own independent research.

In 1950 Stockholm, Sweden, hosted the "First International Conference on Alcohol and Driving." Twenty-two counties participated and the goal was to share information and research and take a substantial first step in making sense of the "problem of alcohol and road traffic." Wagnsson, K., Bjerver, K., Nelker, G., Rosell, S., and Akerbladh-Rosell. *Alcohol and Road Traffic. Proceedings of the First International Conference.* Stockholm: Kugelbergs Boktryekeri. (1951) Although it would appear that there were no definitive answers to the drinking and driving problem, important discussion occurred regarding chemical testing, medical opinions, witness statements, police reports, and how these issues relate to drinking and driving in the legal sphere. Presenters at this conference included authorities on the subject at the time, including L. Goldberg (who presented medical articles regarding the significance of tolerance), R. N. Harger, R. B. Forney and H. B. Barnes (who presented information regarding the estimation of the level of blood alcohol from analysis of breath), and a paper comparing breath analysis and the Widmark method of the determination of ethyl alcohol by K. Bjerver, R.K.

Bonnichsen, and L. Goldberg). *Id.*

New York was the first state to adopt what has commonly become known as the "implied consent law" in 1953. This law was designed to force possible drunk drivers to submit to a blood, breath or urine test after the driver had been stopped by an officer and the officer then had a reasonable belief that the driver was impaired. The theory behind the practice of implementing implied consent laws (also known as informed consent) is that any driver who used the roads and highways implicitly consented to giving his or her permission for a breath or blood (and in some states, urine) sample that could be subsequently used as evidence at trial.

Over the years implied consent statutes have been attacked for a variety of constitutional reasons, usually unsuccessfully. This arena is ripe for litigation but courts have consistently held that the statutes do not violate a driver's Fourth Amendment protection from unreasonable search and seizure, or Fifth Amendment right against self-incrimination. The statutes usually are upheld on due process grounds, although courts have found statutes that permit the revocation of a license without a hearing unreasonable and unconstitutional. In upholding the implied consent laws courts have generally looked to one of two theories supporting their validity. The first theory is that driving on public roads and highways is a privilege, not a right. To be entitled to this privilege a driver must adhere to state laws, including laws prohibiting driving while intoxicated. The second theory is that so long as the driver is afforded due process the implied consent laws are a reasonable regulation of driving pursuant to the state's police power. In hearing arguments that assert that implied consent laws are unconstitutional or unreasonable courts have weighed the interests of society against the interests of individuals, and have ruled that driving under the influence of alcohol or drugs is enough of a danger to society that a slight infringement on the liberty of individuals is justifiable.

The New York law enacted in 1953 enabled a driver to refuse testing but with the penalty of a license suspension of 12 months. Every state has followed the New York law and there is a license suspension or revocation of some length for refusing to provide a breath, blood or urine sample when lawfully requested in every jurisdiction.

Coinciding with the implementation of the New York implied consent law was the introduction of a new breath test machine. In 1954, Robert Borkenstein, a retired Captain in the Indiana State Police who had been the Director of the Police Laboratory, filed for US Patent Number 2824789, "Apparatus for analyzing a gas." He had invented the "Breathalyzer" breath testing instrument.

Coinciding with Borkenstein's invention, President Dwight D. Eisenhower successfully convinced Congress to approve the Interstate Highway System. Eisenhower was inspired by the German Autobahn when his troops occupied Germany during World War II, and more importantly, he understood the immense value to national commerce and travel such a system would create. The Interstate Highway System was authorized by the Federal-Aid Highway Act of 1956 and was popularly known as the National Interstate and Defense Highways Act of 1956. This highway system created changes in mobility for Americans that was unheard prior to the Eisenhower presidency.

The 1950s also saw further studies in the relation of alcohol to road accidents. A controlled study in Toronto, Canada, compared the blood alcohol concentrations of 433 drivers involved in accidents with 2015 other drivers. Lucas, G.

H.W. et al. *Quantitative studies of the relationship between alcohol levels and motor vehicle accidents.* Proceedings of 2nd International Conference on Alcohol and Road Traffic. Toronto. Page 139 (1955) According to the research the danger of accidents became significant when the blood alcohol level was greater than 0.10, and when it rose above 0.15, the hazard was approximately ten times greater than when the concentration was below 0.50. *Id.* A further study in Baltimore, Maryland in 1957 examined 500 consecutive highway fatalities to drivers, passengers and pedestrians. It was determined that approximately one-third of the fatal accidents were associated with blood alcohol levels greater than .150 BAC and about half with levels greater than .50 BAC. Freimuth, H.C., Watts, S. R. and Fisher R.S. *Alcohol and highway fatalities.* J. Forensic Sci. 3, 65 (1957) These figures seem to compare with those reported in a similar survey completed in Perth, in 1957. Pearson, A. T. *Alcohol and fatal traffic accidents.* Med. J. Australia. 2, 166 (1957) Another controlled study of drinking drivers involved in accidents was done in Bratislava, Czechoslovakia. Vamosi, M. *Experiences with non-alcoholic road traffic in Czechoslovakia.* Proceedings of Third International Conference on Alcohol and Road Traffic. London. Pages 79-82 (1963) The results of this study again stated that as a driver's BAC increased so did the hazard. Specifically, the study declared that the chances of being involved in a traffic accident were 124 times greater for a person with a blood alcohol level of over 0.150 than they were for a person with only 0.030. *Id.*

In 1958, the Symposium on Alcohol and Road Traffic at Indiana University declared that a BAC of 0.05 g/dL "definitely impairs the driving ability of some individuals." Levine, Barry. *Principles of Forensic Toxicology.* 2nd Edition. AACC Press

(2006) Further, they claimed that as the BAC increases, an escalating percentage of individuals experience impairment, until the BAC reaches 0.10 g/ dL, at which point all individuals are "definitely" impaired. *Id.* In 1960, the Committee on Alcohol and Drugs issued a statement recommending that DUI laws be amended to reflect a 0.10 g/dL BAC as presumptive evidence of guilt. The Uniform Vehicle Code was amended to reflect this recommendation in 1962.

Along with advances in the study of breath and the ability to capture and evaluate breath samples, further studies were conducted that concentrated on the study of driving under the influence. One of these pre-eminent studies was the "Grand Rapids Study" (Michigan) in 1964. This study examined vehicle accidents and their relation to alcohol use. The study concluded that there was a causal relationship between vehicle accidents and higher BAC levels. Moreover, and more alarmingly, the study showed that there was a higher chance of a fatality when the driver has a higher BAC reading. This report was a precursor to states implementing a lower BAC level for drinking and driving. The first states to actually enact a lower BAC (lower than 0.15%) after the Grand Rapids Study was New York and Nebraska, which did so in 1972.

As the 1960s neared its end the Department of Transportation (DOT) and the National Highway Traffic Safety Administration (NHTSA) began to take a more active role in promoting stiffer legislation for drinking and driving. Their role played on the Grand Rapids study and involved the promotion of statistics proving the connection to fatal automobile accidents and alcohol. Important to mobilizing attention and resources to this perceived problem was the Highway Safety Act of 1966 which effectively federalized this issue by establishing the National Highway Safety Bureau, the precursor of the National Highway Traffic Safety Administration (NHTSA), and by authorizing the U.S. Department of Transportation's historic 1968 report Alcohol and Highway Safety. The 1968 report found that "the use of alcohol by drivers and pedestrians leads to some 25,000 deaths and a total of at least 800,000 crashes in the United States each year." The report warned that "this major source of human morbidity will continue to plague our mechanically powered society until its ramifications and many present questions have been exhaustively explored and the precise possibilities for truly effective countermeasures determined."

In 1970 the federal government decided to solicit bids for research scientists in an attempt to develop a system of standardized "field sobriety tests." The idea behind the government's proposal was to provide police officers tools which would assist in their identification of DUI suspects and their subsequent arrest for suspicion of driving under the influence of alcohol. The National Highway Traffic Safety Administration (NHTSA), a division of the United States Department of Transportation, eventually supported a group of scientists at the Southern California Research Institute (SCRI). Dr. Marcelline Burns, and Dr. Herbert Moskowitz, were the primary authors of the study and the final product, completed in 1983, resulted in NHTSA's "Standardized Field Sobriety Tests (SFSTs)."

The original "SFST Manual" was published in 1984 and was very short and received little attention. Subsequently the NHTSA manuals have been updated over the years with new publications produced in 1987, 1989, 192, 1995, 2000, 2002, 2004 and 2007. These standardized field sobriety tests remain the subject of great debate regarding their validity and the manner in which they are conducted, nevertheless their role in the investigation of DUIs remains an important one.

In the 1960s and 1970s the public's view of drinking and driving was not, arguably, as harsh as it is now. The late Dr. Patricia Waller, a well known advocate for public safety and researcher in the area of drinking and driving, stated that in the past "[d]runk driving was considered more or less a "folk crime," almost a rite of passage for young males. Most adults in the United States used alcohol, and most of them, at some point, drove after doing so. This is not to say that they drove drunk, but many of them undoubtedly drove when they were somewhat impaired." Waller, P.F. Am J Prev Med 21(4, Suppl. 1): 3-4. (2001)

The laws over the years continued to evolve and the pressure on law makers to make DUI laws stricter was too much to ignore. In 1972, Nebraska and New York passed the first laws making driving with a 0.10 blood alcohol content "illegal per se." With this type of law the prosecution need not present any evidence of the driver's impaired ability to drive to support a conviction. These laws were instituted for "public safety" reasons and based on some studies that suggested that drivers were significantly less capable of operating a motor vehicle at this level. By the end of the decade, twelve states had set an illegal per se limit, all of them at 0.10% except New Hampshire which set that state's per se limit at 0.15%. Internationally, other countries enacted per se laws well before the United States. Such laws were introduced in Norway in 1936, Sweden in 1941, Australia in 1966, Great Britain in 1967, and Canada in 1969. Jones, A.W. *Fifty Years on – Looking Back at Developments in Methods of Blood and Breath Alcohol Analysis.* National Board of Forensic Medicine, Department of Forensic Chemistry. University Hospital, SE 581 85 Linköping, Sweden (2000)

A new component to DUI arrests was the "Administrative License Revocation" (also referred to as an "Administrative License Suspension") law and in 1976 Minnesota became the first state to enact such a law. This law had been previously recommended by NHTSA as a manner of suspending or revoking an accused DUI driver's driving privileges regardless of whether the accused had been charged criminally. The idea behind these administrative license suspension laws was that any driver who submitted to a breath test which resulted in a level equal to or greater than the state's presumed "impairment" level would be summarily suspended or revoked for a period of time. Typically the penalties for refusing the breath test were equal to or greater than the penalties imposed if the driver did take the breath test. These laws were civil or administrative in nature in order to avoid any double jeopardy issues.

In 1982 Congress looked to focus some of their attention on the perceived drunk driving problem by passing legislation designed to allocate $125 million to states over a three-year period. The bill was signed into law in December of 1982 and allowed for incentive grants to the states if they adopted the following three legislatively mandated provisions in 23 U.S.C. §101: 1) a 0.10% per se statute; 2) a 90-day license suspension upon probable cause for first-time DUI offenders or those who refuse to take a chemical sobriety test, and 3) a minimum 48 consecutive hours in jail or 10 days community service for subsequent DUI offenses within a five year period.

In addition to the three requirements the states were also mandated to provide increased law enforcement and education efforts designed at eliminating drunk driving. States were also eligible for supplemental funds if they met additional requirements in addition to the basic incentive grants. Although the specific criteria for funding would be determined by federal and state rules, the suggested requirements were that there be: adequate statewide record-keeping regarding drunk driving convictions and license suspensions, alcohol rehabilitation and treatment programs, vehicle impoundment for any person convicted of drunk driving, alcohol safety programs which are financially self-sufficient and locally coordinated, sentence-screening authority by courts, adoption of a 21-year minimum drinking age, and adoption of the recommendations made by the Presidential Commission on Drunk Driving.

Due to intense public pressure President Reagan appointed a National Commission on Drunk Driving, which issued a report recommending a number of ways to enhance the effectiveness of a national anti-drunk driving program. The most significant recommendations of the Commission included selective enforcement and judicially approved roadblocks; the abolition of plea bargaining; victim assistance and restitution programs; administrative per se license suspension; per se statutes; mandatory sentencing; the abolition of pre-conviction diversion; the strengthening of implied consent laws; and increased efficiency in court administration relating to DUI charges.

In 1984 the "Age 21 National Driving Age Law" was enacted to force states to increase the drinking age to 21. Failure to comply would cost those states millions of dollars in federal funds. Several states did initially resist but by 1986 all of the states had complied (Louisiana being the last state to comply).

In 1986 the American Bar Association (ABA) got into the act and formed a national committee to study how to deal effectively, legally and fairly with the drunk driving problem. The ABA National Committee on Drunk Driving was initially focused on the effectiveness, appropriateness and legality of the innovative sanctions and techniques proposed by the Presidential Commission, Mothers Against Drunk Driving (MADD), the National Highway Traffic Safety Administration (NHTSA), the insurance industry and other influential parties. A special Drunk Driving Advisory Project was also formed to evaluate enforcement techniques and alcohol related traffic offenses. The Advisory Project compiled a report entitled, *Drunk Driving Laws & Enforcement: An Assessment of Effectiveness* (1986). Areas that were examined by the Project Advisory Board included roadblocks, per se legislation, preservation of scientific evidence, mandatory jail sentencing and license suspensions, abolition of plea bargaining, a national means to track license suspensions, insurance industry problems, and preservation of due process guarantees in the trial of alleged drunk drivers.

Also in 1986 MADD began its first training of volunteers to support victims of drunk drivers and to serve as "victim advocates" in court proceedings and began to use their influence on a federal level. MADD was founded in 1980 by Candice Lightner after her own personal tragedy of losing her daughter to a DUI accident.

MADD supports education, advocacy and victim assistance in the DUI legal realm and are strong advocates of maintaining the per se blood alcohol content level of .08%, stronger sanctions for DUI offenders, including mandatory jail sentences, treatment for alcoholism and drug dependency issues, the installation of ignition interlock devices, attendance at a victim impact panel (VIP), license suspensions, "sobriety checkpoints" and "saturation patrols," maintaining the legal age of drinking in the United States at 21 years of age, additional taxes on the purchase of beer, and even for lowering the per se BAC limit again to a figure less than the current and accepted limit of 0.08. Without question MADD has been a significant player on the DUI stage, although not without controversy and criticism.

Also around this time a similar organization to MADD was created in England. Campaign Against Drinking and Driving (CADD) was founded by John Knight and Graham Buxton who both lost children to drinking and driving accidents. www.cadd.org.uk

In 1986 the American Medical Association (AMA), who four decades earlier supported per se BAC levels of 0.15%, publicly supported a per se BAC level in the United States of 0.05%. The "Drunk Driving Prevention Act of 1988" was then introduced in 1988 and authorized the Secretary of Transportation, over a period of three fiscal years, to award certain monetary grants to individual states "to improve the effectiveness of the enforcement of laws to prevent drunk driving". *23 USC 410 Under this act* if a state adopted an enforcement program, it received a grant equal to 75% of the cost of implementation and enforcement for the first fiscal year, followed by 50% for the second fiscal year and 25% for the third fiscal year. To be eligible for the federal grant, certain conditions were required including, "an expedited driver's license suspension or revocation system" and "a self sustaining drunk driving prevention program".

In 1990 the United States Supreme Court leapt into action by ruling that "sobriety checkpoints" did not violate the United States Constitution's Fourth Amendment. An individual state was still permitted to protect its citizens from random searches and seizures under their state's constitution, but this was still a huge victory for advocates of roadblocks. *Michigan Dept. of State Police v. Sitz*, 496 U.S. 444, 110 S. Ct. 2481,

110 L.Ed.2d 412 (1990)

In the fall of 1992, the United States Department of Transportation (DOT) issued a report that recommended each state adopt a 0.08% BAC per se statute. The DOT Report concluded, among other things, that "[1]owering the BAC is likely to reduce fatalities....There is also evidence that lowering BACs, and publicizing the effort, can reduce alcohol related deaths at all BACs." In this regard, the Report notes that 80% of the 22,086 alcohol related fatalities in 1990 involved BACs in excess of 0.10%. Whitaker. *DOT Report Recommends States Adopt .08% BAC Per Se Standard.* 7 DWI Journal: Law & Science I (November 1992)

In 1993 the famous "Grand Rapids" study was revisited by a German study sponsored by the Center for Traffic Sciences at the University of Wuerzburg. H.-P. Krüger, H.P., Kazenwadel, J. and Vollrath, M. Grand Rapids Effects Revisited: Accidents, Alcohol and Risk. Center for Traffic Sciences, University of Wuerzburg, Röntgenring 11, D-97070 Würzburg, Germany (1994) This 1993 study addressed the perceived shortcoming in the Grand Rapids Study, namely the risk of causing an accident while the driver was under the influence. The authors of this 1993 study concluded that the 1964 Grand Rapids Study did not know whether the impaired driver was responsible for accidents.

The authors of the German study concluded that their "accident study" replicated the Grand Rapids Study and the "comparison indicates that driving under the influence of alcohol resulted in a greater accident risk in 1994 compared to 1964." Id. The authors also concluded that "simply changing the legal DUI limit from 0.08% to 0.05% is insufficient with respect to alcohol-induced accidents," a most interesting result which seemingly contradicts what MADD and the AMA advocates. Finally, the 1993 study which involved 4,615 accidents and an additional 13,149 motorists, conceded that "although drivers under the influence of alcohol are obviously at a greater relative risk than unintoxicated drivers, the magnitude of the risk to the larger community attributable to the presence of intoxicated drivers remains an unanswered question." *Id.*

In 1995 President Bill Clinton announced that all states needed to adopt the 0.08% per se BAC. Federal legislation was subsequently adopted in October 2000 which threatened to withhold billions of additional federal dollars from states that did not enact new laws implementing the 0.08% per se BAC standard. Most states complied within the next two legislative sessions and in 2005 Minnesota became the final state to pass the law.

In 1998 Congress amended the alcohol-impaired driving incentive grant program which provided extra funding for states that meet certain legislative enactment criteria. In passing TEA-21 (Transportation Equity Act for the 21st Century) a state could qualify for a federal grant by meeting five of seven criteria. The criteria for the basic grant included a program targeting drivers with high BAC levels.

To qualify under the high-BAC criteria states must demonstrate the establishment of a graduated sanctioning system that provides enhanced or additional sanctions (punishments) to drivers convicted of DUI if they were found to have a high BAC. Further, the enhanced sanctions must be mandatory, must apply to the first (and subsequent) DUI offense, and may include longer terms of license suspensions, increased fines and treatment for substance abuse where appropriate.

In the last couple of decades drug DUI cases have been growing in number. More and more American motorists are taking prescribed or over-the-counter medications that cause negative and potentially dangerous effects on the driver. Furthermore, in the last 10 years or so, police officers have been trained on "drug recognition" techniques that assist them in identifying drivers who have taken drugs that impair motor skills. Use of common non-prescription medicine such as aspirin, ibuprophen or acetaminophen can have an additive effect to a person's impairment from alcohol while many non-prescription drugs (ie. antihistamines) can impair a person who later consumes alcohol. This "combination" of alcohol and many types of medications, including prescription and illegal drugs, can drastically increase the impairment effects on a driver. In 2003, Nevada became the first state to pass DUI drugs laws setting presumptive impairment levels for a variety of contraband substances such as marijuana, followed in 2005 by a similar law in Virginia.

The criminalization of a DUI charge is now taking a different road by making a DUI offense a felony. Currently, thirty-seven states have DUI statutes that incorporate a felony charge if the driver has prior DUI convictions.

Although these statutes differ among states, there are some similarities, those being that states use two major factors to determine if the DUI will result in a felony. The first factor, used by all of the felony DUI states, is the number of prior DUI convictions at the time of the offense. The number required to raise a DUI to a felony ranges from the second to the fifth conviction, with the majority of states setting the limit at the third or fourth DUI conviction. The second factor, required by thirty states, is the DUI offender must have a specific number of prior convictions within a certain period of years before the current DUI conviction will be a felony. These time periods range from three to twelve years with the majority of states having either a five or ten year limit. Two states, Idaho and Kentucky, incorporate a third factor in the felony DUI determination. Both states use the BAC level of the driver at the time of the offense to define a felony threshold. These felony convictions also increase the potential jail time facing the individual accused of DUI.

CHAPTER **2**

The DUI Stop and Arrest

The Stop/Contact

The first indicator that a driver may be under the influence usually comes from an officer's observation of the individual's driving (or phone calls from citizens to 911). Moreover, with limited exceptions an officer must observe driving that creates reasonable suspicion of criminal activity or otherwise violates the traffic code before making any contact with the driver. Specifically, the Supreme Court in the seminal case *Terry v. Ohio*, 392 US 1 (1968) stated that a Fourth Amendment prohibition on unreasonable searches and seizures is not violated when a police officer stops a suspect and has a reasonable suspicion that the person has committed, is committing, or is about to commit a crime. Further, this reasonable suspicion must be based on "specific and articulable facts" and not merely upon an officer's hunch. To that end, and again, with limited exceptions, officers must observe specific facts that they can articulate in order to validate a stop.

The National Highway Traffic Safety Administration

(NHTSA) has produced a pocket-size booklet intended primarily for law enforcement entitled Guide for Detecting Drunk Drivers at Night, DOT HS-805-711 (available free of charge from NHTSA, Administrative Operations Division, Room 4423, 400 Seventh Street, N.W., Washington, DC 20590).

In addition to observations made by an officer that rise to reasonable suspicion of criminal activity, an officer may also validate a stop of a vehicle if he observes a simple traffic violation. The following is a list of the driving behaviors and their related indicia of intoxication. The corresponding number is the percentage that the driver has a blood-alcohol concentration of 0.10 percent or higher. *(note: any studies supporting these findings are clearly not scientific and as such, not accepted by the scientific community)*

Turning with Wide Radius	65
Straddling Center or Lane Marker	65
Appearing to be Drunk	60
Almost Striking Object or Vehicle	60
Weaving	60
Driving on Other Than Designated Roadway	55
Swerving	55
Slow Speed (more than 10 mph below limit)	50
Stopping (without cause) in Traffic Lane	50
Drifting	50
Following too closely	45
Tires on Center or Lane Marker	45
Braking Erratically	45
Driving Into Opposing or Crossing Traffic	45
Signaling Inconsistent with Driving Actions	40
Stopping Inappropriately (other than in lane)	35
Turning Abruptly or Illegally	35

Accelerating or Decelerating Rapidly   30

Headlights Off   30

In addition to observing behavior that gives rise to the suspicion of possible criminal activity and/or observing a traffic violation, there is a third way in which an officer can lawfully stop or contact a driver. This falls under the general heading of "community caretaking." The idea behind this principal is that law enforcement is permitted to stop or contact a driver when the officer "wishes to warn a driver about some impending peril," *State v. Chisolm*, 39 Wn. App. 864 (1985) or if the driver is in need of assistance (ie. was in a motor vehicle accident and is injured). However, the community caretaking role is ripe for abuse and when the "officer's concerns have ended, the officer has no further reason to proceed with any additional investigative efforts and the community caretaking function ends." *State v. DeArman*, 54 Wn. App. 621 (1989); *Barrett v. Comm.*, 435 S.E.2d 902 (Va. App. 1993); *State v. Cryan*, 727 A.2d 93 (N.J. Super. 1999)

Probable Cause to Detain

Once an officer has made a lawful stop of the suspected impaired driver, or otherwise has reason to contact the driver, he then will be looking for signs of possible impairment. The initial observations of a DUI driver by an officer typically refer to the driver showing signs of suspected intoxication. These observations include odor of alcohol, slurred speech, red/watery eyes, flushed face and so on. From the beginning of DUI detection researchers have attempted to find a connection between the initial observations and the possible DUI driver. Bogen, Emil M.D. *The Diagnosis of Drunkenness – A*

Quantitative Study of Acute Alcoholic Intoxication. California and Western Medicine: Vol. XXVI, No. 6. Los Angeles (June 1927)

If the officer observes enough to have a reasonable suspicion to legally justify further detention and investigation, he will ask you to step out of the vehicle and possibly perform "voluntary" field sobriety tests (FSTs). Be forewarned that the officer does not require much to request FSTs.

Breath-Alcohol Odor

In DUI cases involving alcohol, which are still the great majority, the odor of alcohol on a driver's breath is one of the first clues an officer relies upon to initially determine that a driver has been drinking. Many studies have been conducted to determine how accurate this particular observation is and no study known to this author has proven the value of alcohol detection by odor in relation to intoxication. In a 1999 study on the ability to detect alcohol use by odor, 20 officers with significant DUI experience were requested to detect an alcohol odor from 14 different individuals with a BAC level of between 0 and 0.13%. The study determined that the officers were unable to determine what alcoholic beverage the subjects had consumed and that the odor strength detected by the officers were unrelated to the subjects BAC levels. Moskowitz, H, Burns, M, Ferguson S. *Police Officers' Detection of Breath Odors From Alcohol Ingestion.* Accid. Anal Prev. 31(3):175-180, Page 175 (May 1999)

In summary, the odor of alcohol does not prove how much alcohol has been consumed. However, the odor of alcohol on a person's breath may permit the officer to continue to investigate the driver for a possible DUI.

Slurred Speech

Another common observation by police officers in DUI arrests is the observation that the driver has slurred speech. A study conducted in 2000 researched the ability for an officer to determine the degree of alcohol impairment (light, moderate and heavy drinkers) of individuals who were asked to speak during a learning phase, when sober, and at four BAC levels (3 ascending curve and one descending). The participants in the study displayed considerable changes in speech as the level of alcohol impairment increased. Importantly the study warned that these speech patterns "cannot be viewed as universal since a few subjects (about 20%) exhibited no (or negative) changes." Hollien, H., DeJong, G., Martin, C.A., Schwartz, R., Liljegre, N. K. *Effects of Ethanol Intoxication on Speech Suprasegmentals.* J Acoust Soc Am.; 110(6):3198-3206, Page 3198. (December 2001) And it is this point that must be emphasized in all DUI cases, that slurred speech cannot be generalized as intoxication.

Not all researchers have agreed that slurred speech or changes in speech is evidence of intoxication. While there are numerous studies that have found that impairment can be determined by slurred speech it is equally true that there are several other studies that have found the opposite. Hollien, H., Liljegren, K., Martin, C.A., DeJong G. *Production of Intoxication States by Actors—Acoustic and Temporal Characteristics.* J Forensic Sci. Jan;46(1):68-73. (January 2001); Pisoni, DB, Martin, CS. *Effects of alcohol on the acoustic-phonetic properties of speech: perceptual and acoustic analyses.* Alcohol Clin Exp Res. 13(4):577-87. (August 1989); Klingholz, F., Penning, R., Liebhardt, E., *Recognition of Low-Level Alcohol Intoxication From Speech*

Signal. J Acoust Soc Am. 84(3):929-35. (September 1988)

Field Sobriety Tests (FSTs)

Once the driver has been detained and there is suspicion of DUI, the officer must then utilize tools at his/her disposal to further detect indicators of impairment. Field sobriety tests have been used throughout the past century by police officers to help them assess whether an individual is too impaired to drive an automobile. These tests were initially not very sophisticated and included the smell of alcohol on the breath, the ability of a person to walk a chalk line, and various behavioral signs and symptoms of inebriation. Prior to NHTSA standardizing field sobriety tests in the 1980s, such tests in the United States had little consistency, no standardization, and as a result questionable reliability: "[b]ecause of the inconsistencies in the experimental procedures and approaches used by investigators, few generalizations regarding the influence of alcohol on performance can be advanced." *The Effect of Alcohol on Human Performance: A Classification and Integration of Research Findings.* American Institutes for Research. Page iv. (May 1973)

NHTSA first published SFST manuals to be used by law enforcement agencies in field sobriety testing in 1981, with revisions to the originals in 1992 (PB 94-780228 Student Manual, PB 94-780210 Instructor Manual), 1995 (AVA-19911BB00 Student Manual, AVA-19910BB00 Instructor Manual) 2000 (AVA-20839BB00 Student Manual, AVA-20838BB00 Instructor Manual), 2002 (AVA-21135BB00 Student Manual, AVA-21134BB00 Instructor Manual), 2004 (Participant and Instructor Manuals, HS 178 R9/04), and most recently in 2006 (Student and Instructor Manuals, HS 178

R2/06). The result was a battery of three standardized field sobriety tests, namely, the horizontal gaze nystagmus (HGN), the walk and turn test, and the one-leg stand.

What you should know

The first thing to know about field sobriety tests (FSTs) is that they are voluntary tests, and are therefore not mandatory. If you are ever asked by a police officer to perform the FSTs, politely refuse. If you refuse to take the test it does, however, become more likely that you will be arrested. But keep in mind that if the officer is requesting that you perform these tests his mind may already be made up.

In addition to the three "standardized" FSTs that are recognized by the National Highway Traffic Safety Administration ("NHTSA"), there are numerous other tests that some officers use as "sobriety tests." However these tests are not recognized as standardized FSTs by NHTSA and if performed should have little or no weight in your criminal case despite what law enforcement likes to think. To be valid, the NHTSA approved tests must be administered and graded precisely according to NHTSA rules for each and every DUI suspect.

Horizontal Gaze Nystagmus (HGN)

The technical definition of nystagmus is that is the rhythmic back and forth oscillation of the eyeball that occurs when there is a disturbance of the vestibular (inner ear) system or the oculomotor control of the eye. There are two major types of eye movements: pendular and jerk. Pendular nystagmus is where the oscillation speed is the same in both directions. Jerk nystagmus is where the eye moves slowly in one direction and then returns rapidly. Most types of nystagmus have the fast and slow phase (jerk nystagmus). Horizontal Gaze Nystagmus (HGN), which is the type of nystagmus used in DUI investigations, is a type of jerk nystagmus with the jerky movement toward the direction of the gaze. Adams, Raymond D. & Victor, Maurice. *Disorders of Ocular Movement and Pupillary Function.* Principles of Neurology. Ch.13, 117 (4th ed. 1991)

Like most types of nystagmus, HGN is an involuntary motion, meaning the person exhibiting the nystagmus cannot control it or is even aware of it. Forkiotis, C.J. *Optometric Exercise: The Scientific Basis for Alcohol Gaze Nystagmus.* 59 Curriculum II, No. 7 at 9 (April 1987); Good, Gregory W. & Augsburger, Arol R. *Use of Horizontal Gaze Nystagmus as a Part of Roadside Sobriety Testing.* 63 Am. J. of Optometry & Physiological Optics 467, 469 (1986); Stapleton, June M. et al. *Effects of Alcohol and Other Psychotropic Drugs on Eye Movements: Relevance to Traffic Safety.* 47 Q.J. Stud. on Alcohol 426, 430 (1986)

Critics of the horizontal gaze nystagmus test for DUI (alcohol) related purposes have argued that alcohol is not the only potential cause of nystagmus and there are many different causes of nystagmus that have been observed and studied. Syndromes such as influenza, vertigo, epilepsy, measles, syphilis, arteriosclerosis, muscular dystrophy, multiple sclerosis, Korsakoff's Syndrome, brain hemorrhage, streptococcus infections, and other psychogenic disorders all have been shown to produce nystagmus. Additionally, conditions such as hypertension, motion sickness, sunstroke, eyestrain, eye muscle fatigue, glaucoma, and changes in atmospheric pressure may result in gaze nystagmus. Pangman. *Horizontal Gaze Nystagmus: Voodoo Science.* 2 DWI J. 1, 3-4 (1987)

Further, these same critics have argued that alcohol is not the only drug to cause nystagmus and that caffeine, nicotine, or aspirin also lead to nystagmus almost identical to that caused by alcohol consumption. *Id.* at 3-4. Finally, conditions such as a person's circadian rhythms or biorhythms can affect nystagmus readings as the body reacts differently to alcohol at different times in the day and even fatigue nystagmus can be found in an individual, and the list, according to critics, goes on. *Id.* at 3-4; Booker, J.L. *End-position nystagmus as an indicator of ethanol intoxication.* Sci Justice. 41(2):113-116. (April – June, 2001)

Administrative Procecures

1. Check for eyeglasses;
2. Verbal instructions;
3. Position stimulus (12-15 INCHES);
4. Equal pupil size and resting nystagmus;
5. Tracking;
6. Lack of smooth pursuit;
7. Distinct and sustained nystagmus at maximum deviation;
8. Onset of nystagmus prior to 45 degrees;
9. Total the clues
10. Check for vertical gaze nystagmus.

Test Interpretation

The Officer should look for three clues of nystagmus in each eye (total of 6 clues).

1. The eye cannot follow a moving object smoothly;
2. Nystagmus is distinct and sustained when the eye is

held at maximum deviation for a minimum of four seconds;

3. The angle of onset of nystagmus is prior to 45 degrees.

Based on the original research, if the officer observes four or more clues it is likely that the suspect's BAC is above 0.10. Using this criterion the Officer, in theory, should be able to classify about 77% of suspects accurately. Obviously these beliefs are only plausible if the field sobriety testing is done in accordance with the NHTSA guidelines. [NHTSA, U.S. Department of Transportation, HS 178 R2/06, *DWI Detection and Standardized Field Sobriety Testing, Student Manual* (2006), p. VIII-7-8]

Walk and Turn

The walk and turn test is a "divided attention" test that is designed to determine the subject's balance, listening skills, and ability to follow instructions. In this test the participant stands in a heel-to-toe fashion with arms at their sides while a series of instructions are given by the officer. Following the instructional phase the suspect must then take nine heel-to-toe steps along a line, turn in a prescribed manner, and then take another nine heel-to-toe steps back along the line. All of this must be done while counting the steps aloud and keeping the arms at the sides. The individual is informed not to stop walking until the test is completed.

NHTSA warns the officer that this test requires a "designated straight line and should be conducted on a reasonably dry, hard, level, non-slippery surface." *DWI Detection and Standardized Field Sobriety Testing, Student Manual.* NHTSA;

U.S. Department of Transportation. HS 178 R2/00, Page VIII-12 (2000) Additionly, the officer is informed in the manual that original research indicated that individuals over the age of 65, and those with back, leg or middle ear problems had difficulty performing the test. Subjects wearing heels more than 2 inches high should be given the opportunity to remove their shoes. *Id.* Over the years however, some of the original instructions and provided information has been deleted from subsequent student manuals.

Administrative Procecures

1. **Instructions Stage: Initial Positioning and Verbal Instructions**

    For standardization in the performance of this test, have the suspect assume the heel-to-toe stance by giving the following verbal instructions, accompanied by demonstrations:

    - "Place your left foot on the line" (real or imaginary). Demonstrate.
    - "Place your right foot on the line ahead of the left foot, with heel of right foot against toe of left foot." Demonstrate.
    - "Place your arms down at your sides." Demonstrate.
    - "Maintain this position until I have completed the instructions. Do not start to walk until told to do so."
    - "Do you understand the instructions so far?" (Make sure suspect indicates understanding.)

2. **Demonstrations and Instructions for the Walking Stage**
   Explain the test requirements, using the following verbal instructions, accompanied by demonstrations:

   - "When I tell you to start, take nine heel-to-toe steps, turn, and take nine heel-to-toe steps back." (Demonstrate 3 heel-to-toe steps.)
   - "When you turn, keep the front foot on the line, and turn by taking a series of small steps with the other foot, like this." (Demonstrate).
   - "While you are walking, keep your arms at your sides, watch your feet at all times, and count your steps out loud."
   - "Once you start walking, don't stop until you have completed the test."
   - "Do you understand the instructions?" (Make sure suspect understands.)
   - "Begin, and count your first step from the heel-to-toe position as 'One.'"

Test Interpretation

According to NHTSA the Walk and Turn test has a maximum of eight clues that are graded and observed by law enforcement. Two clues apply during the "instructional stage" that occurs while the suspect is standing heel-to-toe and listening to the instructions:

- One clue that is observed by the officer is whether the subject fails to keep balance (i.e. suspect breaks away from the heel-to-toe stance). Swaying or using arms for balance is not considered a clue at this point; and

- The second clue observed by an officer prior to the walking stage is whether the subject starts walking too soon (i.e. suspect starts walking before you say "begin").

The remaining six validated clues occur during the walking stage of the test. They are follows:

- Stops walking (i.e. the subject pauses for several seconds).
- Misses heel-to-toe (i.e. more than 1/2 inch gap).
- Steps off the line (i.e. the foot must be entirely off the line).
- Raises the arms while walking (i.e. more than 6 inches).
- Takes the wrong number of steps.
- Turns improperly.

According to NHTSA two or more clues out of a possible eight indicate that the suspect's BAC as above a 0.10%. NHTSA generalizes this finding and does not note a difference in an individual regarding the finding of 2 or 8 clues. [NHTSA, U.S. Department of Transportation, HS 178 R2/06, *DWI Detection and Standardized Field Sobriety Testing, Student Manual* (2006), p. VIII-9-11]

One Leg Stand

The one leg stand test, like the walk and turn field sobriety test, is a divided attention test that is designed to determine the subject's balance, listening skills, and ability to follow instructions. In this test the participant is required to stand on one leg while the other leg is extended in front of the person in a "stiff-leg" manner. This extended foot is to be held approximately six inches above and parallel with the ground. While this is occuring the person is instructed to stare at the elevated foot and count aloud until told to stop, by counting "one thousand and one, one thousand and two, one thousand and three," and so on.

Also like the walk and turn test this test requires a "reasonably dry, hard, level, and non-slippery surface." *DWI Detection and Standardized Field Sobriety Testing, Student Manual*. NHTSA; U.S. Department of Transportation. HS 178 R2/00, Page VIII-12 (2000) Further, the officer has knowledge that original research indicated that individuals over the age of 65, and those with back, leg or middle ear problems had difficulty performing the test. Subjects wearing heels more than 2 inches high should be given the opportunity to remove their shoes. *Id.*

Administrative Procecures

Per NHTSA, the officer is instructed to give the test as follows:

- Tell suspects to stand with feet together and arms down at the sides.
- Tell suspects to maintain that position while you give the instructions; emphasize that they should not try to perform the test until you say to "begin."
- Ask suspects if they understand.
- Tell suspects that when you say to "begin" they must raise their leg in a stiff-leg manner, and hold the foot approximately six inches off the ground, with the toe

pointed forward so that the foot is parallel with the ground.

- Demonstrate the proper one-legged stance.
- Tell suspects that they must keep the arms at the sides and must keep looking directly at the elevated foot, while counting in the following fashion: "one thousand and one, one thousand and two, one thousand and three," and so on until told to stop.
- Ask the suspect if he or she understands.
- Tell the suspect to "begin."

The officer is also given the following instruction:

- It is important that this test last for thirty seconds. You must keep track of the time. If the suspect counts slowly, you will tell him or her to stop when thirty actual seconds have gone by, even if, for example, the suspect has only counted to "one thousand and twenty."

Test Interpretation

The One Leg Stand has four clues of impairment:

- Sways while balancing (side to side or back to front).
- Uses arms to balance (i.e., more than 6 inches).
- Hopping.
- Puts foot down.

Two or more clues classify the subject as a 65% chance of being over a 0.10% BAC. [NHTSA, U.S. Department of Transportation, HS 178 R2/06, *DWI Detection and*

Standardized Field Sobriety Testing, Student Manual (2006), p. VIII-12-13]

Non-Standard Field Sobriety Tests

While the standardized field sobriety tests are now commonplace and regularly practiced by law enforcement when investigating a possible DUI driver, the non-standardized field sobriety tests are still used on a regular basis. Obviously the validity of these tests remain questionable.

Romberg Test

Of all the field sobriety tests that are non-standardized the best known and most commonly used is the Romberg Test. A German ear specialist by the name of Moritz Heinrich Romberg developed a balance assessment test in 1853 that could be used to diagnose diseases. This test is known as the "Romberg Test" and is widely used as a non-specific test of neurological or inner ear dysfunction. The Romberg Test has been modified for use by police officers in the performance of Field Sobriety Tests although this test is not a standardized Field Sobriety Tests. The test is also part of the battery of tests and examinations used in the 12-Step Drug Recognition Examinations, found at the end of this chapter.

The Romberg Test is a neurological test to determine whether a subject can keep a steady standing position with the eyes closed. The basic test has an individual stand with his feet together, hands at his side, head tilted back, and eyes closed. The basic test has developed into several different variations. These different versions are commonly referred to as the "Sharpened" Romberg or the "Modified Position of Attention."

While there have been no studies validating the Romberg test in the DUI context, a number of studies have been conducted concluding that the Romberg Test when performed in the law enforcement environment is unreliable. ImObersteg, A. *The Romberg Balance Test: Differentiating Normal Sway from Alcohol-Induced Sway*. DWI Journal, Law & Science, Vol. 18, No. 5 (May, 2003) Additionally, studies have found that the increased sway found in testing can relate to things other than alcohol intoxication, such as weight, age, physical condition, exercise, sleep loss, elevated temperatures, and antihistamines. Anderson, Theodore E. et al. *Field Evaluation of a Behavioral Test Battery for DWI*. DOT-HS-806-475 (1983)

Finger to Nose

Another commonly used non-standardized field sobriety test is the finger to nose test. This test is a basic test that requires the subject to close his eyes and then touch the tip of his nose with the tip of his index finger, alternating hands. NHTSA research and studies revealed that the finger to nose test, along with the Rhomberg Test, only indicated the presence of alcohol, and "did not increase the predictive ability of testing." Sworn Testimony of Marcelline Burns in *State v. Meador*, 674 So. 2d 826, 834 (Fla. Dist. Ct. App. 1996)

Alphabet, Count Down, and Finger Count Tests

Other non-standardized field sobriety tests that are often used are the alphabet recitation, a numerical count down, and finger count tests. The alphabet test requires the subject to recite part of the alphabet (e.g., starting at a letter other than A and stopping at a letter other than Z). The count down test simply requires the subject to count aloud numbers in reverse, from highest to lowest. For example count backwards from 50 to 30. The finger count test requires the subject to touch the tip of the thumb to the tip of each finger on the same hand in a particular order while counting (e.g., "one, two, three, four—four, three, two, one).

These tests were considered in the initial NHTSA study in 1977 but were discarded and therefore not selected as accurate indicators of alcohol impairment. The Standardized Field Sobriety Test (SFST) Student Manual warns that these techniques are not as reliable as the SFST tests and "do not replace the SFST." NHTSA, U.S. Department of Transportation, HS 178 R2/00. *DWI Detection and Standardized Field Sobriety Testing, Student Manua.* Page VI-4 (2000)

Handwriting

Another test that is not often done by law enforcement but is occasionally used by prosecuting attorneys to indicate possible impairment is handwriting. In a 2003 study the researchers concluded that while handwriting changes can be observed at any level of alcohol, "none of the alterations in handwriting can be attributed to the effects of alcohol intake alone." Asicioglu, F, Turan, N. *Handwriting Changes Under the Effect of Alcohol. Forensic* Sci Int. 8;132(3):201-210. Page 201 (April 2003) Additionally another study concluded that handwriting could not be used in any way to measure accurately the blood alcohol concentration of a writer. Galbraith, NG. *Alcohol: Its Effect on Handwriting.* J Forensic Sci. 31(2):580-588. Page 580 (April 1986)

In summary, there is not a scientific study that has indicated that such a handwriting test has ever been evaluated for reliability as a "sobriety test" to determine alcohol influence or impairment.

Drug Recognition Experts (DRE) History and Development

A drug recognition expert or drug recognition evaluator (DRE) is a police officer who is trained to recognize impairment in drivers who are under the influence of drugs other than, or in addition to, alcohol. The International Association of Chiefs of Police (IACP) coordinates the International Drug Evaluation and Classification (DEC) Program with support from the National Highway Traffic Safety Administration (NHTSA) of the U.S. Department of Transportation.

The Los Angeles Police Department (LAPD) originated the DRE program in the early 1970s after LAPD officers noticed that many of the individuals arrested for driving under the influence had very low or zero alcohol concentrations. The officers suspected that the arrestees were under the influence of drugs but lacked the knowledge and skills to support their suspicions. As a result two LAPD sergeants collaborated with various medical doctors, research psychologists, and other medical professionals to develop a simple, standardized procedure for recognizing drug influence and impairment. Their efforts culminated in the development of a multi-step protocol and the first DRE program. The LAPD formally recognized the program in 1979.

In the early 1980s NHTSA started to take notice of the LAPD DRE. The two agencies worked together to develop a standardized DRE protocol, which led to the development of the DEC Program. During the ensuing years, NHTSA and various other agencies and research groups examined the DEC program and their studies attempted to demonstrate that a properly trained DRE can successfully identify drug impairment and accurately determine the category of drugs causing such impairment. The success of a DRE examination is naturally up for debate, depending on who you ask.

The DRE protocol is, according to the literature, a standardized and systematic method of examining a Driving Under the Influence of Drugs (DUID) suspect to determine whether or not he is impaired and, if so, whether the impairment relates to drugs or a medical condition. Lastly, if the impairment is due to drugs, what category or combination of categories of drugs are the likely causes of the impairment. The advocates of the DRE process believe that the program is designed to be *systematic* because it is based on a set of observable signs and symptoms that are known, according to the program, to be reliable indicators of drug impairment.

The idea of the DRE evaluation is that a conclusion of drug impairment is not based on one particular element but instead on the totality of facts that emerge from the evaluation. Like the SFST program from NHTSA, the DRE evaluation is *standardized* because it is supposed to be conducted the same way, by every drug recognition expert, for every suspect whenever possible. Standardization, in theory, is important because it makes the officers better observers, helps to avoid errors, and promotes professionalism. Naturally this assumes that every DRE is done in exact accordance with the protocol outlined below. The DRE process is also being utilized by law enforcement in Canada and Australia, in addition to the United States.

Arguments against validating drug recognition experts are many and begin with the simple fact that DREs are not medically trained professionals and therefore cannot render a judgment of an individual's impairment based on the criterion provided. Further, the DRE program is usually taught by other law enforcement personnel and not by medical professionals.

The 12-Step DRE Protocol

The DREs utilize a 12-step process in reviewing potential drivers under the influence of drugs. The 12-step process usually requires approximately 30-45 minutes to complete however, the evaluation can take longer depending on the drug ingested. These twelve steps include the following:

1. *Breath Alcohol Test:* The arresting officer reviews the subject's breath alcohol concentration (BAC) test results and determines if the subject's apparent impairment is consistent with the subject's BAC. If so, the officer will not normally call a DRE. If the impairment is *not* explained by the BAC, the officer requests a DRE evaluation.

2. *Interview of the Arresting Officer:* The DRE begins the investigation by reviewing the BAC test results and discussing the circumstances of the arrest with the arresting officer, if he was not the arresting officer. The DRE asks about the subject's behavior, appearance, and driving. The DRE also asks if the subject made any statements regarding drug use and if the arresting officer(s) found any other relevant evidence consistent with drug use.

3. *Preliminary Examination and First Pulse:* The DRE conducts a preliminary examination to determine

whether the subject may be suffering from an injury or other condition unrelated to drugs. Accordingly, the DRE asks the subject a series of standard questions relating to the subject's health and recent ingestion of food, alcohol and drugs, including prescribed medications. The DRE observes the subject's attitude, coordination, speech, breath and face. The DRE also determines if the subject's pupils are of equal size and if the subject's eyes can follow a moving stimulus and track equally. The DRE also looks for horizontal gaze nystagmus (HGN) and takes the subject's pulse for the first of three times. The DRE takes each subject's pulse three times to account for nervousness, check for consistency and determine if the subject is getting worse or better. If the DRE believes that the subject *may* be suffering from a significant medical condition, the DRE will seek medical assistance immediately. If the DRE believes that the subject's condition is drug-related, the evaluation continues.

4. *Eye Examination:* The DRE examines the subject for HGN, vertical gaze Nystagmus (VGN) and for a lack of ocular convergence. A subject lacks convergence if his eyes are unable to converge toward the bridge of his nose when a stimulus is moved inward. Depressants, inhalants, and dissociative anesthetics, the so-called "DID drugs", may cause HGN. In addition, the DID drugs may cause VGN when taken in higher doses for that individual. DID drugs, as well as cannabis (marijuana), may also cause a lack of convergence.

5. *Divided Attention Psychophysical Tests:* The DRE

administers four psychophysical tests: the Romberg Balance, the Walk and Turn, the One Leg Stand, and the Finger to Nose tests. The DRE can accurately determine if a subject's psychomotor and/or divided attention skills are impaired by administering these tests.

6. *Vital Signs and Second Pulse:* The DRE takes the subject's blood pressure, temperature and pulse. Some drug categories may elevate the vital signs. Others may lower them. Vital signs provide valuable evidence of the presence and influence of a variety of drugs.

7. *Dark Room Examinations:* The DRE estimates the subject's pupil sizes under three different lighting conditions with a measuring device called a pupilometer. The device will assist the DRE in determining whether the subject's pupils are dilated, constricted, or normal. Some drugs increase pupil size (dilate), while others may decrease (constrict) pupil size. The DRE also checks for the eyes' reaction to light. Certain drugs may slow the eyes' reaction to light. Finally, the DRE examines the subject's nasal and oral cavities for signs of drug ingestion.

8. *Examination for Muscle Tone:* The DRE examines the subject's skeletal muscle tone. Certain categories of drugs may cause the muscles to become rigid. Other categories may cause the muscles to become very loose and flaccid.

9. *Check for Injection Sites and Third Pulse:* The DRE

examines the subject for injection sites, which may indicate recent use of certain types of drugs. The DRE also takes the subject's pulse for the third and final time.

10. *Subject's Statements and Other Observations:* The DRE typically reads *Miranda*, if not done so previously, and asks the subject a series of questions regarding the subject's drug use.

11. *Analysis and Opinions of the Evaluator:* Based on the totality of the evaluation, the DRE forms an opinion as to whether or not the subject is impaired. If the DRE determines that the subject is impaired, the DRE will indicate what category or categories of drugs may have contributed to the subject's impairment. The DRE bases these conclusions on his training and experience and the DRE Drug Symptomatology Matrix. While DREs use the drug matrix, they also rely heavily on their general training and experience.

12. *Toxicological Examination:* After completing the evaluation, the DRE normally requests a urine, blood and/ or saliva sample from the subject for a toxicology lab analysis.

Drug Categories Evaluated by a DRE

The DRE categorization process is premised on the belief championed by physicians that different types of drugs affect people differently. Accordingly drugs may be categorized or classified according to certain shared symptomatologies or effects, and these drugs are divided into one of seven categories: Central Nervous System (CNS) Depressants, CNS Stimulants, Hallucinogens, Phencyclidine (PCP) and its analogs, Narcotic Analgesics, Inhalants, and Cannabis. It is believed that drugs from each of these seven categories can possibly affect a person's central nervous system and impair a person's normal faculties, and in the DUI field, affect a person's ability to safely operate a motor vehicle.

1. *Central Nervous System (CNS) Depressants:* CNS Depressants slow down the operations of the brain and the body. Examples include alcohol, barbiturates, anti-anxiety tranquilizers (e.g. Valium, Librium, Xanax, Prozac, Thorazine), GHB (Gamma Hydroxybutyrate), Rohypnol and many other anti-depressants (e.g., Zoloft, Paxil).

2. *CNS Stimulants:* CNS Stimulants accelerate the heart rate and elevate the blood pressure and "speed-up" or over-stimulate the body and include Cocaine, "Crack", Amphetamines and Methamphetamine.

3. *Hallucinogens:* Hallucinogens cause the user to perceive things differently than they actually are. Examples include LSD, Peyote, Psilocybin and MDMA (Ecstasy).

4. *Dissociative Anesthetics:* Dissociative Anesthetics are drugs that inhibit pain by cutting off or dissociating the brain's perception of the pain. PCP and its analogs are examples of Dissociative Anesthetics.

5. *Narcotic Analgesics:* Narcotic analgesic relieves pain, induce euphoria and create mood changes in

the user. Examples include Opium, Codeine, Heroin, Demerol, Darvon, Morphine, Methadone, Vicodin and OxyContin.

6. *Inhalants:* Inhalants include a wide variety of breathable substances that produce mind-altering results and effects. Examples of inhalants include Toluene, plastic cement, paint, gasoline, paint thinners, hair sprays and various anesthetic gases.

7. *Cannabis:* Cannabis (marijuana) is a popular drug consumed prior to driving. The active ingredient in cannabis is delta-9 tetrahydrocannabinol, or THC. This category includes cannabinoids and synthetics like Dronabinol.

CHAPTER 3

Breath/Blood Testing

Constitutional Rights (aka Miranda Rights)

If the officer has sufficient facts that would justify a reasonable suspicion that you have been driving under the influence of alcohol, he will arrest you, handcuff you and transport you to the police station for a breath test. At the police station you will be requested to provide a sample of your breath, blood, or urine (in some states). While being transported, the officer may advise you of your Constitutional Rights (*Miranda* rights).

Miranda rights originated from the U.S. Supreme Court case *Miranda v. Arizona*, 384 U.S. 436 (1966). Simply, once the police officer determines that you are under arrest and not free to leave he may question you regarding your driving, your drinking, and anything else regarding the DUI. Importantly however, the officer must advise you of your *Miranda* Rights. Also, he must also make sure that you understand them. *Miranda* Rights are as follows:

1. *You have the right to remain silent and refuse to answer questions. Do you understand?*
2. *Anything you do say may be used against you in a court of law. Do you understand?*
3. *You have the right to consult an attorney before speaking to the police and to have an attorney present during questioning now or in the future. Do you understand?*
4. *If you cannot afford an attorney, one will be appointed for you before any questioning if you wish. Do you understand?*
5. *If you decide to answer questions now without an attorney present you will still have the right to stop answering at any time until you talk to an attorney. Do you understand?*
6. *Knowing and understanding your rights as I have explained them to you, are you willing to answer my questions without an attorney present?*

Some of the most damaging evidence in a DUI case, as in most criminal cases, often comes from the defendant's own mouth: admissions. Although the statements may be spontaneous and therefore unable to be suppressed based on Miranda, they usually come in reply to questions asked by the arresting officer. These questions tend to follow routine and are generally designed to determine what and how much you had to drink.

Typically, the admissions made in a DUI case occur close to when you should be given your Miranda advisements and therefore warned of the danger of making statements. The usual prosecution argument is that although the defendant was not free to leave (which should trigger Miranda), the questioning was part of a preliminary investigation, conducted before the individual had been placed in custody, and thus the advisements were not yet required. In reality the officer usually decides at a very early stage that the suspect was intoxicated and will be arrested, even prior to the preliminary investigation. Prior to the questioning the officer usually has observed such signs of intoxication as erratic driving, alcoholic breath, bloodshot eyes, thick and slurred speech, and staggering out of the car. Even if you choose to say nothing, it is very likely that the officer will arrest you any way. Many of my clients tell me that they make statements hoping to talk their way out of the arrest. This never happens so don't make that mistake.

Implied Consent Warnings (ICW)

The law demands that you be read the implied consent warnings or are advised of the implied consent warnings prior to the administration of a breath or blood test. The implied consent statute provides that any person who operates a motor vehicle is deemed to have given consent to a test or tests of breath or blood (and urine in some states) if arrested for any offense where the arresting officer has reasonable grounds to believe the person had been driving or was in actual physical control of a motor vehicle while under the influence of liquor or drugs.

To be valid the warnings must be timely and to be timely, the warnings must be given in advance of the time you are asked to provide a breath sample. For you to properly decide whether to submit to a breath test, the officer must accurately advise you of the right to refuse the test as well as the consequences of such a refusal. The law states that an implied consent warning is sufficient if it permits "a person of normal intelligence" to understand the consequences of his actions. The warning must only permit the opportunity to make a knowing and voluntary decision.

If the warnings confuse you about your rights under the implied consent statute, you may claim that you had no reasonable opportunity to make an informed decision about whether to take the test. However, you must communicate this confusion to the officer in order to later make such an argument.

Breath Testing (BrAC)

Breath testing in the DUI context has remained the work horse over the years in providing law enforcement with scientific evidence of impairment. Law enforcement has advocated that breath testing remains a relatively reliable form of obtaining the BAC from an individual and furthermore, it remains a relatively inexpensive manner of evidenciary testing. Naturally there is also much criticism regarding the relability of breath testing. *Note: technically a breath test sample uses the acronym BrAC (a blood test sample is a BAC), but courts, police officers, prosecutors and defense attorneys most often refer to breath testing evidences as BAC, and for consistency I shall do the same in this book.*

There is little debate in the DUI community that breath testing is an inferior method of testing an invidivual's blood alcohol concentration in comparison to blood. However, it is equally agreed that breath testing does have some advantages over a blood draw, those primarily being that it is cheaper, faster, gives immediate results, and is less invasive.

The biggest problem with a breath test compared with a blood test is reliability. Since the 1970s, researchers have warned scientists and those who use breath testing devices of factors that can affect a reliable breath alcohol (BAC) reading. Mason, M., Dubowski, K., *Breath-Alcohol Analysis: Uses, Methods, and Some Forensic Problems*. Review and Opinion. J Forensic Sci. (January, 1976) The primary factors that can potentially affect the accuracy of a breath testing machine include physiological factors, machine characteristics, and administrative practices.

The Science of Breath Testing

The general idea behind breath testing is that the breath-test measures the amount of alcohol in a deep-lung breath sample. That amount is then translated to BAC using a chemical analysis using such scientific methods as infrared spectrophotometry, gas chromatography or fuel-cell detection.

With an infrared system, the most commonly used and most advanced of the three above examples, breath is blown into a chamber. Then an infrared beam is shot through the chamber and alcohol molecules are absorbed by the beam. The beam is reduced in size as it passes through the chamber and is then measured. The more light absorbed, the higher the reading on the machine. Computer software then translates the results to a BAC reading.

The resulting ratio computed by the software describes the relationship between breath alcohol content and blood alcohol content. The number that is computed defines the breath quantity that contains the same amount of alcohol as a given blood quantity. The value of 2100:1 is legislatively accepted as the population average and has been almost universally adopted. Translated, this means 2100 parts of breath contain the same quantity of alcohol as 1 part of blood.

The test results that are computed by the breath test machine may also be affected by other issues involving the test subject. These personal issues may include age; lung function, overall strength and size, a disease or condition such as asthma, diabetes, eardrum rupture, ketosis, emphysema, bronchitis, dental issues, fever or harelip, shock or trauma, certain types of special diets, or hiccoughing, burping, vomiting or hyperventilating. Heartburn can make breath results unreliable particularly if the individual suffers from a severe form of acid reflux called GERD (Gastroesophageal reflux disease).

In addition to human (subject) factors that may affect the accuracy of the breath test machine there may also be technical issues that could affect the accuracy of the results. Such technical issues could include (depending on the machine used):

- The machine must be warmed to the correct operating temperature;
- The simulator solution must be kept at 34 degrees centigrade, plus or minus 0.02 degrees; a decrease of one degree will cause a 6.8 percent decrease in the amount of alcohol, resulting in a falsely higher BAC reading for tested breath samples. A thermometer attached to the simulator is supposed to be checked by the operator.
- The sample chamber must be heated to exactly 50 degrees. No variation in temperature is acceptable. This is monitored by the machine's computer.
- The detector must be cooled to a temperature almost to freezing. This is also monitored by the machine's computer.

- The breath tube must be heated to 50 degrees and if not properly heated condensation can form in the tube which can capture alcohol during a test and be picked up by later breath samples. Despite the need for a 50 degree temperature, the Operator's Manual tells the operator only to "check that the mouth piece is warm or hot to the touch."
- An adequately deep lung sample must be ensured;
- The equipment must be maintained properly, calibrated correctly and cleaned adequately;
- Other items such as mouthwash or adhesive, or lip ointment can affect test results (a proper mouth check would likely eliminate this potential problem);
- Police radios may cause radio frequency interference (RFI) with the testing equipment;
- The subject may have had exposure to a gas or vapor such as paint, floor sanding, varnishing or other chemicals;
- Outside environmental causes in the surrounding air may cause inaccurate test results.

The breath test's service guides also list the following possible error messages on the machine's LCD display, which may include:

- Temperature low
- Temperature high
- Printer error
- CRC error
- Pump error
- System won't zero

The breath test machines can be temperamental and on occasion prone to error. While it is not necessary to understand every working component of these machines, it is imperative that your attorney examine the records (available online) of your particular machine to ensure that your machine didn't encounter any malfunctions prior to or after your breath sample was provided.

Evidentiary Breath Test Devices

Like most things in DUI law, there is little consensus regarding which breath testing machine is superior. As such different states use different machines. However, the four most common brand names, in order or popularity are the Intoxilyzer, BAC Datamaster, Intoximeter, and Draeger. All of these devices use similar technology, namely infrared light that passes through a sample chamber (where the breath is passing through) and/or electrically charged "plates" (fuel cell devices) which attract and "count" ions of alcohol as their "measuring" tool.

STATE	BAC EQUIPMENT USED
Alabama	Draeger 7110 Phasing Out Intox 5000
Alaska	Datamaster & Intox 3000
Arizona	Intox 5000
Arkansas	Datamaster
California	Everything Datamaster
Colorado	Intox 5000
Connecticut	Intox 5000
Delaware	Intox 5000

Florida	Intox 5000
Georgia	Intox 5000
Hawaii	Intox 5000
Idaho	Alcosensor III, Intox 5000
Illinois	EC/IR, Intox 3000, Intox 5000, 1400
Indiana	Datamaster
Iowa	Intox 4011 & Datamaster CDM
Kansas	Intox 5000
Kentucky	Intox 5000EN
Louisiana	Intox 5000
Maine	Intox 5000 + Balloon Kits
Maryland	EC/IR
Massachusetts	Datamaster & Intox 5000
Michigan	Datamaster
Minnesota	Intox 5000EN
Mississippi	Intox 5000
Missouri	Datamaster, Intox 5000, + Others
Montana	Intox 5000
Nebraska	Intox 5000 & 4011
Nevada	Intox 5000
New Hampshire	Intox 5000
New Jersey	Breathalyzer
New Mexico	Intox 5000 & RBT IV
New York	Datamaster & Intox 5000
North Carolina	Intox 5000
North Dakota	Intox 5000
Ohio	Datamaster, Intox 5000, Verifier
Oklahoma	Intox 5000
Oregon	Intox 5000

Pennsylvania	Intox 5000 Mix - Datamaster and RBT IV
Rhode Island	Everything
South Carolina	Datamaster
South Dakota	Intox 4011 ASQ (Quartz)
Tennessee	EC/IR, 5000, 1400
Texas	Intox 5000
Utah	Intox 5000
Vermont	Datamaster
Virginia	Intox 5000
Washington	Datamaster, Draeger
Washington DC	Intox 5000
West Virginia	Intox 5000
Wisconsin	EC/IR
Wyoming	Intox 3000, EC/IR, Alcosensor IV

Once you arrived at the police station or mobile BAC unit, you will eventually be offered to take a chemical test of your breath. If you refuse to submit to chemical testing you will undoubtedly be charged with a DUI. If you provide a breath sample and it reads above 0.08 you will almost certainly be charged with a DUI. In some cases you may be charged with DUI even if your breath sample is below 0.08.

The breath test can only determine the BAC at the time the test is taken, which may be higher or lower than when the vehicle was actually operated. Evidence of the BAC at time of driving is often presented in the form of "retrograde extrapolation," a questionable process whereby earlier blood alcohol levels are estimated by applying a formula developed in 1932 known as "Widmark's formula." However, all states give a period of time when the breath test must be taken in order to prove the driver was "per se" driving under the influence. The time in most states (and Washington) is two hours, although other states allow the officer to obtain the BAC reading within three hours of driving. If the breath test is not obtained within this prescribed period it does not mean that the State or City cannot prove that you drove under the influence by using the BAC results. However, the prosecuting attorney must also prove that you were in fact impaired which results in a potentially more difficult case for the prosecuting attorney (particularly if the BAC was not extreme).

Blood Testing

A blood draw in lieu of a breath test is an option available in many states. Blood draws, when performed properly, are generally more accurate. However, even if the blood draw is an "option," it may not be *your* option!

In many states, including the State of Washington, a blood draw is an alternative to a breath test if you are under arrest for vehicle homicide, vehicular assault, if you are unconscious (and were arrested for DUI, physical control, or minor under the influence), or a DUI arrest resulting from an accident with serious bodily injury. The other way that a blood draw may be administered is if you are physically unable to provide a breath sample (ie. asthma, emphysema).

States usually require that no person other than a physician, registered nurse or a phlebotomist qualified by the state can draw the blood for purposes of determining the alcohol concentration. However, there is a move afoot where some states are experimenting with allowing law enforcement to administer blood draws. I personally cannot think of anything more frightening that having an angry and perhaps medically unqualified law enforcement officer drawing blood from my arm. However, it would also be ripe for legal attack. Each state has specific guidelines stating how these tests are to be taken, transported, preserved, secured, and analyzed.

Such guidelines and procedures must be used to collect the blood sample, otherwise the blood analysis will be flawed. For example, the American Medical Association suggests the following procedures:

1. Hypodermic needles and syringes (must) be sterile and disposable. When reusable equipment is utilized, it should neither be cleaned with nor stored in alcohol or other volatile solvents.

2. Only a chemically cleaned, dry tube or vial with inert stopper should be used. Neither alcohol nor volatile solvents should be used to clean them. The tubes and vials should contain an anticoagulant (recommended are fluoride, citrate, oxalate and heparin), and a preservative (recommended are fluoride and mercury salt.) See American Medical Association, *Alcohol and the Impaired Driver: A Manual of the Medical-Legal Aspects of Chemical Tests for Intoxication with Supplement on Breath/Alcohol Tests* (1976 reprint).

The anticoagulant in the vial is designed to prevent the sample from clotting inside the vial. The preservative prevents yeast growth, which may cause the blood to ferment, thereby increasing the concentration of ethyl alcohol in the sample. Finally, the sample should be refrigerated during storage with 1% sodium fluoride. Lesser concentrations may allow microorganisms to grow, thereby inhibiting glycolysis. *See* Kaye,

"The Collection and Handling of Blood Alcohol Specimen," 75 American Journal of Clinical Pathology 743 (1980).

Areas of concern or inquiry as to the validity of the blood sample include:

- The collection of the blood sample by the nurse, doctor or phlebotomist;
- Use of an appropriate blood collection kit;
- The transportation of the blood;
- The storage of the blood;
- The preparation of the blood for testing;
- The testing of the blood;
- The chain of command in handling the blood;
- The reporting of the blood alcohol level.

Blood Specimen Collection – the Legal Checklist

The officer (god help you) or phlebotomist drawing the blood from a suspect should follow the steps noted below in order to ensure the specimen will be accurately analyzed and the chain of custody will be intact. Any significant deviation from these steps may raise questions about the accuracy of the sample analysis.

Step One: Remove all components from the blood alcohol kit box.

Step Two: Assemble needle to holder.

Step Three: Apply tourniquet and prepare venipuncture site using only a non-alcoholic antiseptic. *Note:* Some antiseptics contain alcohol as a solvent.

Step Four: Following normal hospital/clinic procedure, withdraw blood specimen from subject. The arm should be in a downward or lowered position, while the tube should be in a slanted position with the stopper in the highest position.

Step Five: As the tube begins to fill, the tourniquet should be removed. The contents of the tube should not contact the stopper. Special attention should be given to the arm position in order to prevent possible backflow from the tube and the possibility of adverse reaction to the subject.

Step Six: When the tube fill is complete, blood should cease to flow. The tube should be removed from the holder and any additional tubes should be placed into the holder following the same procedure.

Step Seven: When sampling is completed, the needle/holder assembly should be removed in its entirety. A dry, sterile compress should be applied to the venipuncture site. The arm should be elevated.

Step Eight: To assure proper mixing of the chemicals in the tube with the blood, each tube should be slowly and completely inverted at least five times immediately after blood collection. *The tube should not be shaken vigorously.*

Step Nine: The subject's name or other identifying information should be placed on the tube.

Step Ten: Any paperwork associated with the blood kit must be filled out and signed by the person withdrawing the blood.

Step Eleven: The blood tubes should be properly packaged and placed in the blood kit. A liquid-absorbing packet should be included with the test tubes to determine if any leakage occurs during transportation.

Step Twelve: A biohazard label should be affixed to the exterior of the blood kit. The kit is now ready for transportation to the laboratory for analysis.

Note: Normally, a complete toxicology screen requires two tubes of blood (20 ml)

CHAPTER 4

DUI Court Procedures

Bail

Bail is a process through which you are permitted to pay money in exchange for your release from police custody, usually after booking or sometimes after the arraignment if the Judge demands that you are taken into custody. As a condition of release, you must promise to appear in court for all scheduled court dates - including arraignment, pre-trial hearings, readiness hearings, motions, and the trial itself.

If you are not allowed to post bail at the police station immediately after booking, a judge may decide later, at a separate hearing or the arraignment, whether to allow release on bail. The bail amount may be predetermined, through a "bail schedule," or the judge may set a monetary figure based on:

- Your DUI record and criminal history;
- Seriousness of the DUI offense, in terms of injury to others;
- Your ties to family, community, and employment.

If bail is imposed you or your friends and family may "post" the full bail amount as set by the court, or a "bond" may be posted in lieu of the full amount. A bond is a written guarantee that the full bail amount will be paid if you fail to appear as promised. Bonds are usually obtained through a bail bond agency that charges a fee for posting of the bond (usually about 10 percent of the bail amount). Bail bond agencies may also demand additional collateral before posting the bond, since the agency will be responsible for paying the full bail amount if the suspect "jumps bail" and fails to appear as promised.

If you are arrested, booked, and granted release on your own "personal recognizance," no bail money needs to be paid to the court, and no bond is posted. You are then released after promising, in writing, to appear in court for all upcoming proceedings. Most state criminal courts impose certain conditions on personal recognizance release, which include not driving unless you are properly licensed and insured, not consuming alcohol or illegal drugs, and not refusing a breath test if lawfully requested. Additionally, there may be additional conditions such as attendance at AA meetings or getting an alcohol/drug evaluation within a prescribed time limit.

If you are released on your own "personal recognizance" and subsequently fail to appear in criminal court as scheduled, you will be subject to immediate arrest.

The Arraignment

The arraignment is your first appearance in court and may occur as soon as the next available court date after your arrest, or in some instances you will be notified by mail (summons) with the arraignment date. In situations when you are notified by mail the date might be within a couple of weeks of your arrest or several months later, depending on the jurisdiction of your DUI. The arraignment is mandatory, hence you must appear. The first appearance is primarily for the advisement of rights and your opportunity to declare "not guilty." If you have an attorney, he will advise you of the proper procedures. You should always request a jury trial (you can change your mind later, if you so wish) and naturally, always plead not guilty.

At the conclusion of the arraignment, the Judge will decide whether any conditions should be imposed on you. For first time offenders with relatively low breath or blood test results, the typical conditions include no driving unless you are licensed and insured, no driving after drinking, or no consumption of alcohol or non-prescribed drugs pending trial. For those with prior offenses, or relatively high breath test results, the conditions can include additional penalties such as the installation of an ignition interlock device, installation of a SCRAM bracelet, the requirement of probation monitoring, or the burden of significant bail. Check with your attorney on what to expect as some Judges impose "pre-trial conditions" that may not be lawful.

One relatively recent case regarding reasonable pretrial conditions was decided in Washington State, namely *Butler v. Kato*, 137 Wn. App. 515, 524 154 P.3d 259 (2007) The court referenced a court rule (CrR 3.2) that gave guidance to what conditions of release are reasonable. Namely, the court rule stated that the court may impose certain conditions on a defendant to ensure public safety, including prohibiting the accused from committing any violations of criminal law, possessing or consuming intoxicating liquors, requiring the posting of a bond, and imposing travel restrictions or electronic monitoring. However, pre-trial alcohol evaluations and

AAs are not permitted and thus the court cannot lawfully impose such conditions (at least in Washington).

It is important to note that there is a risk that you will be taken into custody during your arraignment, particularly if you are a repeat offender. Hence, having a lawyer present will help your cause tremendously. After the arraignment you will be given notice to appear for a pre-trial hearing.

The Pre-trial Hearing

The pre-trial hearing (sometimes referred to as the "readiness hearing") is typically the second scheduled court date and is scheduled at your arraignment and is usually several weeks after your arraignment, depending on the court. The pre-trial is intended to provide an opportunity for your lawyer and the prosecutor to discuss the case (pros and cons), explore plea bargaining options, and to determine whether the parties have exchanged all information required by court rules.

Continuances of the pre-trial hearing are not uncommon. Typically, pre-trials are continued because the defense needs to:

- Obtain court ordered information, such as police radio tapes, toxicology reports, documents relating to the breath test, accident reconstruction reports, missing pages from police reports, etc.;
- Complete witness interviews;
- Complete independent investigations;
- Retain an expert witness;
- Locate missing witnesses;
- Obtain alcohol evaluations;
- Prepare a Deferred Prosecution;

- Conduct additional negotiations with the prosecutor; and/or
- Continue for the presentation of a disposition (the parties may have an agreement but need more time to prepare).

If no continuance is needed and no acceptable plea bargain has been offered, your attorney may note (schedule) various legal motions (to argue the validity of certain evidence – see next paragraph) or confirm a trial date.

The Motion Hearing

The motion (or suppression) hearing can be the most important hearing in your defense, because it is at the motions hearing that the judge will hear legal challenges to the admissibility of the State/City's evidence, and a ruling in your favor can result in evidence being suppressed (excluded) from your trial, including evidence of a blood or breath test, the results of some or all of the field sobriety tests, or any adverse statements you may have made. Successful pre-trial motions often compel the prosecutor to make an advantageous plea bargain offer, or on occasion, result in the dismissal of the charge!

Most courts schedule the motions hearing for a date well in advance of the trial. Some courts, however, schedule most motions for the morning of trial. Most Judges will rule on motions immediately.

The Trial

The length of a DUI jury trial is typically two days. It may be as short as a day if there is no blood or breath test, and if there are few witnesses, but rarely does it last three days or more.

The Court will first hear preliminary matters (motions in limine) which are followed by the jury selection (called voir dire). This is the process whereby both sides ask the potential jurors questions to determine their biases, views on police, DUIs, etc., and to enable each to excuse up to three jurors.

Once the jury is selected both your lawyer and the prosecuting attorney give opening statements where they outline for the jury what they expect the evidence to show. The defense attorney may choose to give his or her opening statement after the prosecutor has rested his or her case.

The prosecutor then presents his or her witnesses which typically include:

- Investigating police officers;
- Civilian witnesses or hospital personnel that may be available and favorable to the prosecution;
- "Expert witnesses" from the State Patrol breath test department or the state's toxicology lab, both of whom will testify that the breath testing device was operated and maintained in accordance with all required state statutes and regulations governing breath testing; or
- In a blood draw case, the person who drew the blood and the toxicology lab technician who analyzed the blood will be called.

At the conclusion of the prosecutor's case, the defense may, but is not required to present evidence. In most cases, much of the defense has already been presented through the defense attorney's vigorous cross-examination of the prosecution witnesses.

Typical defense witnesses include:

- People you were with prior to being stopped by the police who can testify to the amount you had to drink, your apparent state of sobriety, unimpaired coordination, speech and appearance;
- Passengers in your car who can testify to the above plus your driving and performance of the roadside tests;
- People you may have called from your car after the stop or from the police station who can testify to your speech;
- The public defender or other lawyer you called from the station who can testify to your speech, the appropriateness of your questions and your ability to understand and follow instructions;
- Anyone you called or who saw you after release who can testify to your sobriety, coordination, speech and appearance;
- Any experts retained to challenge the accuracy/reliability of the breath or blood test;
- Defense investigators who have interviewed prosecution witnesses, including the arresting officer, photographed or videotaped the road traveled and the scene of the field sobriety tests, or who is an expert on the limitations of "field sobriety testing;" and
- The defendant does have the option to testify, but cannot be required to. Most juries want to hear from the defendant personally, but there may be sound reasons your attorney will recommend against testifying. While the decision rests with the defendant, the defense attorney's advice should be considered very carefully.

After all the evidence is presented, the judge instructs the jury as to what the law is that they are expected to apply to the facts of the case. Then both lawyers present closing arguments.

Following the closing argument, the jury will have the opportunity to discuss the case (deliberate) and this can last anywhere from 15 minutes to one or more days. Only three outcomes are possible at this juncture:

1. All six jurors can vote to acquit and the case will be over and the matter dismissed;
2. All six jurors can vote to convict and the defendant will be found guilty; or
3. The jurors can deadlock without reaching a unanimous verdict. This is called a "hung" jury and the judge will declare a mistrial. The prosecutor then has the option of re-trying the case at a future date, offering a plea bargain to a reduced charge, or dismissing the case.

DUI Sentencing

If you are convicted of DUI, whether after a guilty plea or a jury verdict, the appropriate legal punishment is determined at the sentencing stage. A number of different kinds of punishment may be imposed on a person convicted of DUI, including:

*   Payment of fines and costs (statutory and probation costs)
*   Jail
*   Probation

- Suspended sentence (for 5 years)
- Suspension of driver's license
- Community service
- Drug/alcohol evaluation and treatment or alcohol/ drug information school (ADIS)
- DUI Victim's Panel
- Ignition Interlock Device (may be mandatory)

Sentencing usually takes place almost immediately after a DUI conviction, with the sentencing judge receiving input from the prosecutor and the defense. In some instances a judge may give you a new court date for sentencing. There are some judges who demand you complete an alcohol evaluation prior to the imposition of sentence (another good reason to obtain the evaluation early).

For sentencing purposes a judge may consider the following:

- Your criminal history and any prior convictions for DUI
- Level of intoxication and your behavior
- Impact of the DUI on any victims (i.e. whether injuries or passengers)
- Your personal, economic, and social circumstances
- Your regret or remorse that you express
- The agreement between you and the prosecuting attorney

Probation

A consequence of a criminal conviction is probation. The purpose of probation is to monitor the individual to ensure compliance of the sentencing conditions, such as completion of an alcohol evaluation, alcohol treatment, payment of fines, and maintaining lawful conduct.

If you fail to comply with the conditions imposed at sentencing the court may summons you to appear to explain your failure to comply. There are some instances when the failure to comply is relatively minimal and can be corrected prior to your court appearance. In other instances the failure to comply may be severe (i.e. new DUI arrest) and the punishment that results may be harsh (i.e. 30 days or more of jail).

DUI Appeals

If you have been found guilty at trial of a DUI you may "appeal" your case and request that a higher court review certain aspects of the case for legal error, as to either the conviction itself or the sentence imposed. Importantly, you must initiate the appeal within 30 days of the finding of guilt. If you plead to a DUI (or any other offense) you will waive your right to appeal.

In an appeal, you argue that there were key legal mistakes which affected the jury's decision and/or the sentence imposed and that the case should be dismissed or that you should be re-tried or re-sentenced.

In considering an appeal, the court reviewing the case looks only at the "record" of the proceedings in the lower court and does not consider any new evidence. The record is made up of the court reporter's transcripts (or court recordings) of everything said in court, whether by the judge, the attorneys, or witnesses. Anything else admitted into evidence, such as documents or objects, also becomes part of the record. This is why it is critical that your attorney present a solid case and a sound record for later review.

CHAPTER 5

DUI Penalties & Conditions

Jail

Criminal penalties for a DUI depend on a BAC reading (or refusal to provide a breath sample), whether you have prior DUI convictions, and the state where your DUI occurred. The mandatory minimum penalties for DUIs are prescribed by the State Legislature and prohibit judges from going lower than the predetermined penalties.

Regardless of the mandatory minimum penalties you should not assume that the judge will necessarily sentence you to these minimum penalties. A judge always has the discretion to impose up to the maximum penalty permitted by law. You may be sentenced to more than the mandatory minimums if there are factors in your case that would warrant a judge to impose a greater penalty. These factors include, but are not limited to, having passengers in the car (it is worse if the passengers are minors), if you have prior DUIs but they occurred more than seven years ago, if there was an accident, if you were highly belligerent to the police officer, and so on.

Importantly, if you were incarcerated after you were arrested for the DUI you may be given credit for time served, assuming you served more than 24 hours in jail.

Sentencing Enhancements

A sentencing enhancement refers to a situation or fact in your case that the prosecutor and/or judge will potentially use against you to increase the penalties if you are convicted. Facts that could be considered to enhance your punishment (meaning, more jail to serve) would include:

- a child (or any passenger) in the vehicle;
- excessive speed;
- an exceptionally high BAC reading (over 0.15);
- refusing to submit to a blood or breath test;
- an accident, property damage, or injury arising out of the DUI;
- prior related offenses.

Work Release

Work release is an alternative to jail that permits you to work during the day and then return to jail in the evening. You must get permission from the judge and then must be approved by the local corrections facility (or probation department) to participate in the work release program. You will be charged by the day for this privilege. The catch is that typically you must be sentenced to at least 10 days in jail (15 days in jail in some jurisdictions) before you become eligible to apply for work release. This may not be an option in some courts so discuss this option with your attorney prior to sentencing.

Electronic Home Monitoring

Electronic home monitoring (EHM) is "electronic jail" that is served in your home and is imposed at the discretion of the Judge if you are convicted of DUI. If EHM is granted by the judge, you must still "qualify" for it by means of an application through the jail where it is ordered to be served. Generally, the jail administrators screen out persons they feel pose "problems" or "risks."

The availability of EHM as an alternative to jail is dependent on jurisdiction, so it's important that your attorney be familiar with the court and the prosecuting attorney and their practice when it comes to EHM. If EHM is not permitted as an alternative to jail as an option for the court there may be another way to petition the court to grant EHM. A judge may grant EHM as an alternative to jail if the defendant has medical needs that make jail time impractical (for the defendant and jail staff) or medically harmful. In some States EHM is mandatory in addition to jail time. This is only the case for a repeat offender.

EHM uses a computerized box which is attached to your telephone (so you need a land line phone) which establishes a radio link with an electronic ankle bracelet you are required to wear while in detention. Some EHM devices are more sophisticated than others and also may require alcohol breath testing without notice. The most sophisticated devices have the capability to use voice recognition technology and Global Positioning Satellites (GPS) to constantly track, record and report your location. All EHM devices monitor your movements and if you walk beyond a prescribed distance, the computer calls the central monitoring computer and "reports" a violation. EHM is not free and if permitted you will pay for such a "privilege." There is a cost for EHM so please consult with your attorney.

It is likely that EHM will likely continue to grow in use as the technology increases in sophistication, decreases in price, the cost of confinement in jail continues to rise, and the punishment continues to increase for a conviction for DUI. Additionally, the number of people filling the jails continues to increase and jurisdictions are eager to find alternatives to filling the jails.

Community Service

Community service for DUI offenders was developed in the 1980s as an alternative to jail because of high jail costs and limited available space. Whether community service is permitted is ultimately up to the presiding judge.

Once you qualify for community service and it has been approved by the judge, you will be provided a jail commitment date and the opportunity to complete the community service prior to the commitment. If you successfully complete the community service you will not need to appear for your jail commitment. On the other hand, if you do not complete the community service you will still need to appear.

Community service involves working at a not-for-profit organization. Depending on the court, you may be limited to specific organizations to serve your community service. Be sure to check with the court, or better yet, have your attorney check into this. If the court does not demand that you do community service at their designated organizations be sure to get organized early as it often takes time to plan. Typically, organizations that would be approved include the Salvation Army, Food Banks, Food Kitchens, City Parks and Recreation,

Library's, and so on. You will need to provide proof of your service to the court after you complete the hours. Proof should be on the not-for-profit's letterhead and signed by an executive of the organization.

Work Crew

Work crew is an alternative sentencing program that is designed to reduce jail overcrowding by providing minimum risk offenders a work option to meet court obligations. If the jurisdiction in which you are charged permits work crew, you must first qualify and be referred to the work crew program from the court. To qualify for the program you will be screened first to ensure that you qualify. Once you qualify you will be assigned work and your work will be monitored to ensure that you complete all of the assigned tasks. It is important to know the jurisdiction where your DUI occurred as some offer work crew in lieu of jail while others do not.

DUI Victim Impact Panel

Another requirement of probation that is generally imposed at sentencing is a DUI victim impact panel. While this is not a mandatory requirement, practically speaking every judge imposes this sanction. The DUI victim impact panel is a community meeting where volunteers who have been victims, offenders, and witnesses of DUIs give testimonies regarding their experiences they have endured due to the actions of drivers under the influence. The panel's focus is to encourage people to be responsible for their choices. It goes without saying, but it still must be said, you must be completely sober when attending.

MADD (Mothers Against Drunk Driving) has advocated for many years the mandatory attendance at a victim impact panel (VIP) for those charged with a DUI. Most DUI VIPs charge for participation and some of the money collected from fees paid by participants eventually find its way back to MADD. In fact the organization collected $4,436,481 in 2006 from VIPs.

There have been mixed reviews over the years regarding the value of the DUI VIP. Some groups believe that they have tremendous preventative value while others believe that they are valuable to the recovery of victims. According to the John Howard Society, some studies have shown that allowing victims to give testimony is psychologically beneficial to them and aids in their recovery and in their positive opinion of the criminal justice system. *Victim Impact Statements.* John Howard Society of Alberta (1997) In the alternative, a New Mexico study suggested that DUI VIPs tended to be perceived as confrontational by multiple offenders. According to the study such offenders then had a higher incidence of future offenses. Woodall, W.G., Delaney, H., Rogers, E. & Wheeler, D.R. *A Randomized Trial of Victim Impact Panels' DWI Deterrence Effectiveness.* Center on Alcoholism, Substance Abuse, and Addictions (CASAA), University of New Mexico (2000) Overall the effects and overall value of victim impact panels on recidivism has been mixed. Shinar, D., and Compton, R.P. *Victim impact panels: Their impact on DWI recidivism.* Alcohol Drugs Driv 11(1):73-87, (1995); Fors, S.W., and Rojek, D.G. *The effect of victim impact panels on DUI/DWI rearrest rates: A twelve-month follow-up.* J Stud Alcohol 60(4):514-520 (1999); C'de Baca, J., Lapham, S.C., Paine, S., and Skipper, B.J. *Victim impact panels: Who is sentenced to attend? Does attendance affect recidivism of first-time DWI offenders?* Alcohol Clin Exp Res 24(9):1420-1426 (2000)

Ignition Interlock Device

The ignition interlock device (IID, or breath alcohol ignition interlock device (BIID)) is gaining popularity in governmental circles, court systems, and advocates against the crime of driving under the influence. The device is a breath test type apparatus that is connected to the vehicle's dashboard, or more correctly to its ignition mechanism. The instrument requires the driver to provide a breath sample before allowing the vehicle to start. If the breath sample renders a clean result (i.e. a blood alcohol concentration reading below the permitted amount (usually, 0.00, 0.02, or 0.04 per cent) the vehicle's engine will start. Alternatively, if the driver provides a breath sample that is over the required amount then the vehicle will not turn over and the failed attempt will be reported to the governing agency.

While the vehicle is in motion (or the engine is turned on) the IID will randomly require the driver to provide another breath sample. The time between required breath samples is dependent on the calibration of the unit, however typically random breath samples are required every 10 to 20 minutes while the vehicle is in operation. The purpose behind the random breath sample is to prevent a driver from having a "sober" friend blow into the device starting the vehicle. If the requested breath sample is not provided or exceeds the required limit, the device will record the incident, warn the driver and then start up an alarm (e.g., lights flashing, horn honking, etc.) until the ignition is turned off, or a clean breath sample has been provided.

A common, but inaccurate belief is that interlock devices

will turn off the vehicle's engine if alcohol is detected. Due to the fact that this would then create an unsafe or dangerous driving situation that would expose interlock manufacturers to substantial liability, a vehicle's engine does not turn off if a breath sample detects too much alcohol on a driver's breath. It is physically impossible for an interlock device to turn off a running vehicle.

The devices keep a running record of the activity on the unit and this record, or log, is printed out or downloaded each time the device's sensors are calibrated, commonly at 30, 60, or 90-day intervals. In the DUI realm these records are provided to the courts for probation review and to the Department of Licensing in some instances. If the court still has jurisdiction and a violation is detected the court may require the driver to re-appear and possibly face addition sanctions.

Most states in the U.S. now permit judges to order the installation of an IID as a condition of probation. There are also many states that mandate that an IID be installed for repeat offenders and in some states for first offenders. Forty-seven states and the District of Columbia have laws allowing the installation of alcohol ignition interlocks on the vehicles of offenders. Fell, James C., Voas, Robert B., McKnight, A. Scott, and Levy, Marvin. *A National Survey of Vehicle Sanction Laws for Alcohol-Related Driving Offenses in the United States: Preliminary Findings.* Pacific Institute for Research & Evaluation, Calverton, MD National Highway Traffic Safety Administration, Washington, DC. Seattle, Wa. (2007) (the 2007 report listed 43 states plus DC, but in 2010 the number of states with IID laws is 47). A list of federally-approved IID devices is maintained by the National Highway Traffic Safety Administration's NHTSA Conforming Products List.

Secure Continuous Remote Alcohol Monitor (SCRAM)

The "Secure Continuous Remote Alcohol Monitor system," or more commonly known as SCRAM, is a water and tamper-resistant Bracelet that collects, stores and transmits measurements of an individual's blood alcohol content (BAC). The SCRAM device is made by a company named AMS, was developed in 1991, first introduced in 2003, and now is used in more than forty states.

The device is considered a transdermal alcohol sensor and measures alcohol that is lost through the skin from sweat. The device utilizes three technologies that work simultaneously, yet separately, namely the transdermal Alcohol Content (TAC) for alcohol detection, as mentioned, thermometer for determination of body temperature of the subject, and infrared signal system for detection of distance from the skin to the SCRAM unit. The gadget, worn as an ankle Bracelet, "sniffs" every 30 minutes and transfers data via a wireless connection to a probation officer or other law-enforcement official. The device can also detect tampering. This device is used frequently in courts where Judges impose conditions of release after an arraignment or preliminary hearing or by probation departments after sentencing.

Restitution

Restitution is money that you would pay if there was any physical damage that resulted from your arrest and charge for DUI. For example, if there was an accident you must provide proof that either you paid for all the damages that you were liable for (or the insurance deductible). If there is a plea agreement that results in a criminal conviction, whether it be the original charge or DUI or a lesser offense, or if you enter into a deferred prosecution, the court will have the ability to order that you pay restitution. If the amount of restitution is known, you must pay this amount within a prescribed period of time (typically 30 to 90 days). If the amount of restitution is not known, the court will request that the prosecuting attorney contact the victim and request an amount (with supporting evidence) to be forwarded to the court. The court will demand that the amount of restitution is provided to the court within a certain amount of time, typically within 30 to 90 days of the order. If the prosecutor fails to provide the court with this information you will not have to pay the restitution. On the other hand, if the amount of restitution provided appears to be too much and you dispute the amount, you will be afforded the ability to request a "restitution hearing" to argue the validity of the amount.

Insurance

If you are convicted of a DUI (or your license was suspended in the administrative hearing) you will be required to obtain SR-22 automobile liability insurance for a period of at least three years.

When you are eligible to have your license reinstated you go to the Department of Licensing and make an application for reinstatement. The SR-22 form must be taken to your insurance company who then completes the form and mails it directly to the Department of Licensing. The insurance company acknowledges responsibility for reporting any lapse in insurance coverage directly to the Department of Licensing, which may result in an additional suspension of your driver's license.

There are restrictions that coincide with this type of insurance. Such restrictions include the ability to drive only specific cars that are actually included in the policy. Practically speaking, however, the biggest effect that SR-22 insurance has is increased insurance costs. How much more is dependent on your age, the type of car being insured, driving record, type of coverage, limits of coverage, and the insurance company itself. The higher risk, and therefore higher cost, refers to the fact that the insurance is covering a convicted DUI driver. The requirement of having high-risk insurance for a period of at least three years is one of the harshest economic consequences of being arrested for DUI.

Costs

The fines that you are required to pay for a DUI or a lesser offense are, unfortunately, only part of the story. You may also potentially be responsible for the Laboratory Assessment Fee to fund the State's toxicology laboratory; an emergency response fee; filing and conviction fees; and finally, there will be probation costs that can be extraordinarily expensive.

DUI penalties

State	Jail – 1ˢᵗ/2ⁿᵈ /3ʳᵈ (days)	License Suspension - 1ˢᵗ /2ⁿᵈ/3ʳᵈ (days)	Temp. License during Susp.	IID Ignition Interlock Device	Enhanced Penalty	DUI Statute
AL	0/5/60	90 / 1 y/ 3 y	No	No	--	AL Code 32-5A-191
AK	72 h/ 20/ 60	90 / 1 y/ 3 y	Yes	Yes	0.16	AK Statutes 28.35.030
AZ	1/120	90 /90 / 90	Yes	Yes	0.15	ARS Title 28 Chapter 4
AR	1 / 7 / 90	120 / 24 m/ 30 m	Yes	Yes	0.18	AR Code Title 5, Ch. 65
CA	48 hr/ 96 hr / 120	4 m/ 2y/ 3y	Yes	Yes	0.16	California Vehicle Code Sections 23152 - 23229.1
CO	2/ 45/	3 m/ 1 y/1 y	Yes	Yes	0.17	CRS 42-4-1301
CT	48 hr/ 120/ 1 yr	1y/ 3y/ permanent	Yes	Yes	0.16	GSC section 14-227a
DE	0/60 / 1 yr	3 m/ 1 y/ 18 m	No	Yes	0.16	DE Code Title 21 section 4177
DC	0/5 /10	90/ 1y/ 2ys	Yes	Yes	0.15	DC Code section 50-2201.05
FL	0/10 /30	6m/ 1y/ 2ys	Yes	Yes	0.20	FS 316.193
GA	10 / 90/ 120	1y/ 3y/ 5y	Yes	Yes	0.15	Georgia Code 40-6-391
HI	2 / 5 / 10	3m/ 1y/ 1-5y	Yes	Yes	0.15	HRS Chapter 291-E
ID	0/ 10/30	90/ 1y/ 1y	Yes	Yes	0.20	ID Statutes section 18-8004
IL	0/ 5 / 10	90/ 1y/ varied	Yes	Yes	0.20	625 ILCS 5/11-500 to 5/11-505
IN	5 / 10 /	180/ 180/ 180	Yes	Yes	0.15	Indiana Code 9-30-5
IA	48 hr/ 7/ 30	180/ 1y/ 2y	Yes	Yes	0.15	Iowa Code 9-30-5
KS	48 hr/ 90/90	30/ 1y/ 1y	No	Yes	--	KS Statutes Ch. 8, Article 10
KY	2 / 7 / 30	30/ 1y/ 2ys	--	Yes	0.18	KRS Chapter 189A
LA	0/30 / 1 y	90/ 1y/ 2y	Yes	Yes	0.15	LRS 32:661
ME	30/180/271	90/ 18m/ 4ys	Yes	Yes	0.15	MRS Title 29-A section 2411
MD	0/5/10	60/ 120/ --	Yes	Yes	--	MD Transp. Code section 21-902
MA	0/60 / 180	1y/ 2y/ 8y	No	Yes	0.20	90 MGL section 24
MI	0/5 /1 yr	6m/ 1y/ --	--	Yes	--	MI Vehicle Code 257.625-626c

MN	0/30 / 30	90/ 180/ 1y	Yes	Yes	0.20	MN Statutes Chapter 169A
MS	0/5 /1 yr	90/ 2y/ 5y	No	Yes	--	MS Code 63-11-30
MO	24 hr/ 7 / 30	30/ 1y/ 1y	No	Yes	0.15	MRS 577.010 to 5770.54
MT	24 hr/7/ 30	6m/ 1y/ 1y	--	Yes	0.18	MCA Title 61, Ch. 8, Part 4
NE	0/10 / 30	90/ 1y/ 1y	Yes	Yes	0.15	R.R.S. Nebr. § 60-6, 196
NV	2/10 / 1 y	90/ 1y/ 3y	Yes	Yes	0.18	NRS 484.379
NH	0/10 / 180	6m/ 3y/ 5y	No	Yes	0.16	NH Statutes 265:82
NJ	0/2 / 180	3m/ 2y/ 10y	--	Yes	--	NJ Statutes 39:4-50
NM	0/96 hr/ 30	90/ varied/ varied	Yes	Yes	0.16	NMS 66-8-102
NY	0/5/10	90/ 6m/ 6m	Yes	Yes	0.18	NY Vehicle & Traffic Code Article 31
NC	1/7/7	60/ 60/ 90	Yes	Yes	0.16	NCGS 20-138.1
ND	0/ 5/60	91/ 1y/ 2y	Yes	Yes	0.18	ND Code Chapter 39-08-01
OH	3/10/30	6m/ 1y/ 1y	Yes	Yes	0.17	ORC Ch. 4511.19-197
OK	10/1 y/ 1 y	30/ 6m/ 1y	Yes	Yes	0.15	OK Statutes Title 47-11-902v1
OR	2/2/2	90/ 1y/ 1y	Yes	Yes	--	OR Vehicle Code Ch. 813
PA	0/ 5 / 10	1y/ 1y/ 1y	--	Yes	0.16	PA Vehicle Code Ch. 38
RI	0/ 10 / 2 y	45/ 1y/ 2y	--	Yes	0.15	RI Code 31-27
SC	2/ 5 / 60	6m/ 1y/ 2y	--	Yes	0.14	SC Code 56-5-2930
SD	2/2/60	30/ 1y/ 1y	--	No	0.17	SD Codified Laws Ch. 32-23
TN	48 hr/ 45/ 120	1y/ 2y/ 3y	--	Yes	0.20	TN Code section 55-10-401
TX	48 h/10 / 1,500 h	90/ 180/ 180	Yes	Yes	0.15	Texas Penal Code, Ch. 49.04)
UT	48 h/ 10 / 1,500 h	90/ 1y/ 1y	No	Yes	0.16	UT Code 41-6a-502
VT	0/60hr/100 hr	90/ 18m/ permanent	No	No	--	23 VSA section 1201
VA	0/20/ 90	1y/ 3y/ 3y	No	Yes	0.20	VA Code 18.2-266
WA	1/30/90	90/ 2y/ 3y	Yes	Yes	0.15	RCW 46.61.502
WV	0/6 m/ 1 y	6m/ 1y/ 1y	Yes	Yes	--	WV Code 20-7-18b

| WI | 0/ 5 / 30 | 6m/ 1y/ 2y | Yes | Yes | -- | WI Code Chapter 346.63 |
| WY | 0/7/30 | 90/ 1y/ 3y | Yes | Yes | -- | WY Statutes 31-5-233 |

Insurance Institute for Highway Safety, Highway Loss Data Institute, January 2007

CHAPTER 6

Alcohol/Drug Evaluations, Classes, and Treatment

In the context of driving under the influence, alcohol and drug use is front and center. While the great majority of DUI offenders are not substance abusers who require treatment, for those who are there exists another very real dilemma, reoffending. As a result most courts will order the defendant charged with DUI to undergo an alcohol/drug evaluation to determine whether they suffer from substance dependency. Moreover, advocates such as MADD vigorously campaign for mandatory alcohol or drug evaluations in the court environment.

Many pundits have claimed that substance use disorders are a significant public health problem in many countries. Further, the most commonly abused substance is alcohol. Gabbard: *Treatments of Psychiatric Disorders.* Published by the American Psychiatric Association: 3rd edition (2001) As an example, the number of 'dependent drinkers' in the United Kingdom was calculated as over 2.8 million in 2001. *Global Status Report on Alcohol 2004.* WHO European Ministerial Conference on Young People and Alcohol. World Health

Organization: Department of Mental Health and Substance Abuse. Geneva (2004) Additionally, the World Health Organization (WHO) estimates that about 140 million people throughout the world suffer from alcohol dependence. *Id.*

The legal system in America is designed to provide more severe penalties on repeat DUI offenders than first time offenders. However, despite the threat of enhanced penalties for repeat offenders there are a group of individuals who continue to drink then drive. This group is considered the "hard core drinking driver" (HCDD) and according to some, is an individual who despite education, threats, and punishments, drives frequently after consuming alcohol. Simpson, H. M., Beirness, D. J., Robertson, R. D., Mayhew, D. R., & Hedlund, J. H. *Hard core drinking drivers.* Traffic Injury Prevention. *5*(3), 261-269 (2004) This group is in the minority of all impaired drivers but they are a concerning minority to be certain. Recent surveys suggest that 3% of all licensed drivers account for 80% of the total number of impaired driving incidences. *Id.* Because this activity poses relatively high threats to public safety the legal system has attempted to identify individuals in this highest risk category and develop special monitoring and management strategies based on their unique characteristics. Voas, R. B., & Fisher, D. A. *Court procedures for handling intoxicated drivers.* Alcohol Research and Health. *25*(1), 32-42 (2001)

Defining Alcoholism

Attempts to define alcoholism have been met with uncertainty, conflict, and ambiguity. Definitions have evolved from classical-historical times to the present, reflecting the prevalent cultural, religious, and scientific biases. Today the word "alcoholism" simultaneously denotes competing conceptions of the nature and causes of alcohol addiction. These conceptions include moral, legal, medical, behavioral, psychological, and sociological models of alcoholism.

The multiplicity of definitions for alcoholism has proven a barrier to communication among clinicians and researchers, and according to many professionals, a hindrance to effective treatment. Accurate diagnosis is the first step in predicting the course and outcome of a disease, in planning for its treatment, and in comparing the effectiveness of different kinds of treatment. Accurate diagnosis requires unambiguous terminology.

Although they differ in detail and emphasis, most definitions of alcoholism recognize the condition of people who cannot help repetitively drinking quantities of alcohol, usually enough to cause intoxication, which harm them. Before the invention of the term "alcoholism," this condition was designated by a variety of terms, including intemperance, inebriety, and habitual drunkenness.

In 1849, Dr. Magnus Huss, a Swedish physician, first used the term "alcoholism" to describe a diseased condition resulting from excessive alcohol consumption. Coombs, Robert H. *Addiction Counseling Review: Preparing for Comprehensive, Certification, and Licensing Examinations*. Routledge Pub. Page 84 (2004) In 1866, a French doctoral candidate, M. Gabriel, first used the term in its modern sense, as a disease manifested by a loss of control over alcohol intake, leading to excessive alcohol consumption--what we would now refer to as an addiction. *Id.* He also designated alcoholism a public health problem. The use of "alcoholism" to designate a disease identified by the symptom of excessive alcohol intake promptly caught on and was adopted into most modern languages.

Alcoholism was first recognized as a disease in 1785, by the Philadelphian Dr. Benjamin Rush, signer of the

Declaration of Independence and first physician-general of George Washington's Continental Army. In his widely distributed essay on "the effects of ardent spirits," Rush explicitly called intemperance a disease and, explicitly, an addiction. *Id.* Throughout the 19th century, American physicians considered and treated alcoholism (then termed intemperance or inebriety) as a disease. Such examples include the medical journal essays of Dr. J.H. Kain (1828) and Dr. R. Hills (1849) Equally relevant is the founding of special hospitals for the treatment of this disease, as well as special journals for its explication. Among these journals are the *Quarterly Journal of Inebriety* (U.S., 1876-1913), and the *British Journal of Inebriety*, now the *British Journal of Addiction* (1884-present).

Despite the scientific view among many professionals that alcoholism was indeed a disease, there remained widespread doubt, especially among those who attached a moralistic conception of alcoholism. This may best be illustrated by the Reverend J.E. Todd's 1882 essay, *Drunkenness a Vice, Not a Disease.* The essay is replete with quotes connecting alcoholism and sin and here is but one example: "If there is any man on earth who deserves the abhorrence of mankind and the curse of God it is the drunkard." Todd, J.E. Rev. *Drunkenness a Vice, Not a Disease. Hartford*, CT: Case, Lockwood & Brainard. Page 11 (1882) Regardless, the vast majority of physicians, as represented through medical organizations, continue to regard alcoholism as a disease.

Alcohol addiction was recognized in the Standard Classified Nomenclature of Disease produced in 1933 with the explicit approval of the American Medical Association, the American Psychiatric Association (APA), the Association of American Physicians, the American Public Health Association, and the American Hospital Association. Alcoholism is listed in The Manual for Coding Causes of Illness, published by the U.S. Public Health Service in 1944. Logie , H.B., ED. *A Standard Classified Nomenclature of Disease.* New York: Commonwealth Fund (1933)

Diagnostic Criteria for Alcoholism

Like the evolution of the definition of alcoholism the diagnostic criteria for alcoholism has similarly evolved. By definition medical diagnostic criteria for alcoholism assumes that alcoholism is actually a "disease." Therefore, these criteria acknowledge that alcoholism is an addiction, recognized by such symptoms of addiction as withdrawal and increased tolerance. Different sets of criteria place more or less emphasis on these symptoms and many medical definitions and criteria refer to a variety of medical, social, or other adverse consequences associated with alcoholism.

In 1960, E.M. Jellinek noted that some people "who never become addicted" to alcohol were being labeled alcoholics. Jellinek, E.M. *Alcoholism, a genus and some of its species.* Canadian Medical Association Journal 83:1341-1345 (1960); *The Disease Concept of Alcoholism.* Highland Park, NJ: Hillhouse Press. (1960) Jellinek began experimenting with a definition of alcoholism as "any use of alcoholic beverages that causes any damage to the individual or society or both," but immediately noted that this definition was too vague. *Id.* He therefore proceeded to adopt a family of Greek-letter designations for subtypes of alcoholism, only two of which (gamma and delta) refer to true alcohol addiction, and therefore to alcoholism as a disease. Essentially, gamma alcoholism refers to loss of control during drinking bouts, while delta alcoholism refers to inability to abstain (i.e., craving between bouts).

The remaining three categories (alpha, beta, and epsilon) are designed to describe the condition of problem drinkers, not of persons with the disease alcoholism.

DSM-I and DSM-II (1952 and 1968)

The Diagnostic and Statistical Manual of Mental Disorders (DSM), published by the APA, is a diagnostic guide for psychiatric, including addictive, disorders. Subsequent versions of the initial model are still in use today to diagnose those individuals who are obtaining alcohol and drug evaluations for court purposes. The first edition (DSM-I) defined alcoholism as alcohol addiction. American Psychiatric Association, *Diagnostic and Statistical Manual of Mental Disorders* (DSM-I). Washington, DC (1952) The second edition (DSM-II) divided alcoholism into three subcategories, only one of which was characterized as alcohol addiction; the other two categories related to "excessive drinking," or what one might call "problem drinking." American Psychiatric Association. *Diagnostic and Statistical Manual of Mental Disorders,* Second Edition (DSM-II). Washington, DC (1968) The DSM-II definition of alcoholism was based on the definition appearing in the International Classification of Diseases. World Health Organization. *Manual of the International Statistical Classification of Diseases, Injuries, and Causes of Death.* 8th Revision (ICD-8). Geneva: the Organization (1967)

DSM-III and DSM-III-R (1980 and 1987)

The third edition of the DSM model defined alcohol dependence in much the same way as Jellinek had defined gamma alcoholism. American Psychiatric Association. *Diagnostic and*

Statistical Manual of Mental Disorders, Third Edition (DSM-III) Washington, DC (1980). DSM-III criteria for alcoholism requires evidence of either tolerance or withdrawal symptoms, along with evidence of either loss of control, or social or physical problems due to alcoholism. These criteria were kept as consistent as possible with the ninth revision of the ICD. World Health Organization. *Manual of the International Statistical Classification of Diseases, Injuries, and Causes of Death,* 9th Revision (ICD-9). Geneva (1977)

The study and treatment of alcohol dependence continued to evolve and the 1987 revision of DSM-III (DSM-III-R) incorporated a broadened conception of dependence derived from the alcohol dependence syndrome as defined by G. Edwards. Edwards, G. *The alcohol dependence syndrome: A concept as stimulus to enquiry.* British Journal of Addiction 81(2):171-183 (1986).

Alcohol dependence, as defined in the DSM-IV, is a "psychiatric diagnosis and depicts a physical dependence on alcohol." For a person to meet criteria for Alcohol Dependence within the criteria listed in the DSM-IV, they must meet 3 of a total 7 possible criteria within a 12 month period of time.

The first two criteria listed in the DSM-IV are related to physiological dependence: to wit, tolerance and withdrawal. The third and fourth criteria establish a pattern of losing control of drinking by breaking rules/laws or failing at attempts to restrain from drinking. The fifth and sixth criteria are indicative of a progression of addiction as more and more time is spent drinking and the subsequent lifestyle changes that result. The seventh criteria for alcohol dependence is achieved when an individual continues to drink despite being conscious that their drinking is causing or aggravating a particular psychological or physiological problem(s).

Importantly, because only three of seven criteria are required to be diagnosed with alcohol dependence, not everyone evaluated and diagnosed with alcohol dependence meets the same criteria. Therefore not all have identical symptoms and problems connected to drinking. Alcohol dependence is differentiated from alcohol abuse by the presence of symptoms such as tolerance and withdrawal.

The DSM-IV (the standard for diagnosis in psychiatry and psychology) defines alcohol abuse as "repeated use despite recurrent adverse consequences." VandenBos, Gary R. ed. *APA Dictionary of Psychology.* 1st Ed. Washington: American Psychological Association (2007) It further defines alcohol dependence as alcohol abuse combined with tolerance, withdrawal, and an uncontrollable drive to drink. (See DSM diagnosis below.)

The DSM models have not been without critics. The most fundamental criticism of the DSM concerns the validity and reliability of its diagnostic categories and criteria. Kendell, R. and Jablensky, A. *Distinguishing between the validity and utility of psychiatric diagnoses.* Am J Psychiatry (2003); Baca-Garcia, E, Perez-Rodriguez, M.M., Basurte-Villamor, I, Fernandez del Moral, A.L., Jimenez-Arriero, M.A., Gonzalez de Rivera, J.L., Saiz-Ruiz, J, and Oquendo, MA. *Diagnostic stability of psychiatric disorders in clinical practice.* Br J Psychiatry. (2007); Pincus et al. *Clinical Significance and DSM-IV.* Arch Gen Psychiatry (1998) Further, critics have argued that the DSM models lack hard science. Criticism has even come from some of the earlier contributors to the DSM, numerous scientist and mental health professionals, and from politicians.

The next version of the DSM is DSM-V and is tentatively scheduled for publication in 2012. *DSM-V: The Future Manual.*

This as yet unpublished manual has already received criticism. Robert Spitzer, the head of the DSM-III task force, has publicly criticized the American Psychiatric Association for mandating that DSM-V task force members sign a nondisclosure agreement, effectively conducting the whole process in secret: "When I first heard about this agreement, I just went bonkers. Transparency is necessary if the document is to have credibility, and, in time, you're going to have people complaining all over the place that they didn't have the opportunity to challenge anything." Carey, Benedict. *Psychiatrists Revise the Book of Human Troubles. New York Times* (December 17, 2008)

American Society of Addiction Medicine (1990)-ASAM

The new kid on the block in defining and treating addiction is the American Society of Addiction Medicine. American Society of Addiction Medicine. *Disease definition of alcoholism revised. Addiction Review* 2(2):3 (1990) In 1990 ASAM proposed a definition which incorporated many of the then contemporary ideas, namely:

> Alcoholism is a primary, chronic disease with genetic, psychosocial, and environmental factors influencing its development and manifestations. The disease is often progressive and fatal. It is characterized by continuous or periodic impaired control over drinking, preoccupation with the drug alcohol, use of alcohol despite adverse consequences, and distortions in thinking, most notably denial.

The ASAM Patient Placement Criteria -ASAM-PPC

The American Society of Addiction Medicine Patient Placement Criteria (ASAM-PPC) was developed to provide a standardized treatment matching tool that has been in use since the early 1990's. The ASAM criteria allows a "clinician to systematically evaluate the severity of a patient's need for treatment along six dimensions, and then utilize a fixed combination rule to determine which of four levels of care a substance abusing patient will respond to with the greatest success." Turner, W. M., Turner, K. H., Reif, S., Gutowski, W. E., & Gastfriend, D. R. *Feasibility of multidimensional substance abuse treatment matching: Automating the ASAM Patient Placement Criteria.* Drug and Alcohol Dependence (1999) The four levels of care are: Outpatient Treatment (level 1), Intensive Outpatient/ Partial Hospitalization (level 2), Medically Monitored Intensive Inpatient Treatment (level 3), and Medically Managed Intensive Inpatient Treatment (level 4).

Self Reporting

There are several tools that are used by treatment providers to detect whether an individual may have substance abuse issues or may potentially have substance abuse issues. One such tool involves self reports, typically in the form of questionnaires.

The CAGE questionnaire is one such example and has been extensively validated for use in identifying alcoholism. It is not valid for diagnosis of other substance use disorders, although somewhat modified versions of the CAGE are frequently implemented for such a purpose.

Another example of self reporting is the Alcohol Dependence Data Questionnaire which is a more sensitive diagnostic test than the CAGE test. This particular test helps distinguish a diagnosis of alcohol dependence from one of heavy alcohol use.

Yet another self reporting aid is the Michigan Alcohol Screening Test (MAST). This test is used as a screening tool for alcoholism and is used by courts in many jurisdictions to determine the appropriate sentencing for people convicted of alcohol-related offenses. Vaillant, GE. *A 60-year follow-up of alcoholic men.* Addiction. 98: 1043–51 (2003)

The World Health Organization developed its own screening questionnaire called the Alcohol Use Disorders Identification Test (AUDIT). This test is unique in that it has been validated internationally and is commonly used in six countries. Ewing, JA. *Detecting alcoholism. The CAGE questionnaire.* JAMA : The Journal of the American Medical Association 252 (14): 1905–7 (October 1984) Similar to the CAGE questionnaire, it uses a simple series of questions and a resulting high score earns a more thorough investigation of potential issues and dependency.

The last self reporting test of note for alcohol is the Paddington Alcohol Test (PAT) which was developed to screen for alcohol related problems for those who have been admitted into Accident and Emergency departments. It is very similar to the AUDIT questionnaire but with one very significant difference, it is administered far quicker (one-fifth of the time needed for the AUDIT questionnaire). This is an obvious need for individuals who maybe injured or in a trauma like condition.

In addition to alcohol screening tests there are also drug screening tests that are used regularly in the substance screening demanded by the court system. The most widely used drug screening test is the Drug Abuse Screening Test (DAST), developed in 1982. Fundamentally it parallels the Michigan Alcoholism Screening Test (MAST).

At the end of this chapter is a copy of the Michigan Alcohol Screening Test (MAST) and The Drug Abuse Screening Test (DAST), which are most commonly used in determining alcohol and/or drug dependence by State Certified Alcohol/Drug Treatment facilities. It would be very wise to review both prior to being screened by an alcohol/drug treatment provider.

Mandatory Alcohol/Drug Evaluations

Mandatory alcohol/drug evaluations and treatment of DUI offenders to address potential substance abuse problems has support in law enforcement, in the judiciary, and organizations such as MADD. The idea is that if the offender is evaluated, found in need of treatment, and thereafter is treated for substance abuse issues then the chance of repeating the crime of DUI is diminished. Wells-Parker, E., Bangert-Drowns, B., McMillen, R. & Williams, M. *Final results from a meta-analysis of remedial interventions with DUI Offenders. Addiction.* 90:907-926 (1995)

Completing an alcohol/drug evaluation may be compulsory for you if you have been arrested for DUI, regardless of the eventual outcome. It is essential that you do not randomly choose a treatment center. This is an area where direction from your attorney is critical.

Regardless of whether the evaluation is court ordered or if you do it on your own you must be evaluated by a certified counselor in an alcohol program approved by the department of social and health sciences. The evaluation is typically two hours in length and involves your participation in the self reporting questionnaires (MAST and DAST) and an interview with the alcohol/drug counselor. The face to face interview may involve the counselor asking you follow up questions from the questionnaires or alternatively asking you questions about your family history (regarding relatives who may have had substance abuse problems) and your general drinking (or drug use) patterns.

As mentioned, you must get the evaluation from a certified facility. There is no list of approved agencies in this book because the list is voluminous. Also, it is best to get a referral from your attorney because there are some treatment agencies that are better than others. It is important to remember that these agencies are businesses and they make most of their money from treatment, hence there is a willingness by many to quickly recommend treatment when perhaps it is not necessary. Also, your attorney can recommend certified treatment agencies so you do not waste your time and money attending a non-certified treatment facility

When you go to the evaluation you will be required to bring the following information:

- A copy of your five-year driving abstract or record, which is available at your nearest state patrol or department of licensing office;
- A copy of your police report and BAC ticket (describes the "what, why, when, and where's" of your arrest); and
- A copy of any court orders or citations.

The alcohol evaluation is to determine whether you are alcohol dependent and whether you should receive alcohol treatment. The alcohol treatment facility will then prepare a treatment recommendation for the court. If you sign a release form giving permission for the treatment provider to release a copy of the evaluation, a copy will be provided to your attorney, the court and the Department of Licensing (if applicable). It is my firm recommendation that you only sign a release to your attorney who can first review the evaluation to confirm that it is accurate and reflects your combined expectations. Based on this diagnoses and recommendation, the court must order an offender to complete either an approved alcohol drug information school (ADIS) or a more intensive treatment program. See below for more details on ADIS.

If you are evaluated you must be evaluated in accordance with the criteria that has been outlined by the bureau of alcohol and substance abuse within the department of social and health services. There are three categories of evaluation and corresponding treatment:

1. No significant problem (NSP);
2. Significant problem level 1 (SP1); or
3. Significant problem level 2 (SP2).

SP1 indicates a finding of alcohol abuse, while SP2 is a finding of alcoholism. For a defendant evaluated as NSP, alcohol information school will be recommended. For a defendant evaluated as SP1, a treatment program up to one-year in length will be recommended, and for the defendant evaluated as SP2, a treatment program up to two-years in length will be recommended.

It is very important to remember that if convicted of a DUI (or related offense) the court will order that you follow whatever the treatment facility recommends. In other words, even if you are diagnosed as NSP, you must nevertheless complete at least the alcohol school (this is a minimum requirement).

The costs for treatment vary and some insurance companies will pay for a portion of the treatment. Other insurance plans may not cover any of the treatment while a few will pay for the entire treatment plan.

While these long-term treatment plans are generally tailored to the individual's need they are still governed by D.S.H.S. guidelines. The typical 2-year intensive outpatient treatment plan consists of about two to three months of meetings 3-5 times per week. These meetings consist of one-on-one meeting with a counselor, group meetings with other individuals in the treatment facility, attendance at Alcoholics Anonymous, or some other alcohol support group. The intensive two to three month phase is then followed by approximately six months of once per week meetings. The remainder of the two year program involves once per month meetings.

Alcohol and Drug Information School (ADIS)

Alcohol and Drug Information School (ADIS) is an 8-16 hour program (depending on the state) designed to educate the participants about the dangers of alcohol and drugs. This program must comply with the statutory requirements set forth in each state's administrative code or equivalent. ADIS is typically recommended by a treatment provider for those who are deemed to have no significant problem (NSP) with alcohol or drugs.

ADIS includes the following topics:

- Expectations, Pre-test, Choice
- Blood Alcohol Concentration

- Long Term Affects of Alcohol & Drug Abuse
- Patterns of Use, Nonuse, Social Use, Misuse, Abuse and Addiction
- Underage Drinking and Driving
- Washington Penalties
- Financial and Personal Losses
- Breaking the Family Cycle
- Exploring Values / Making Decisions
- Change Plans and Post-test

Alcohol and Drug Support Organizations

It is recognized that most people who are arrested and charged with driving under the influence have simply made a solitary mistake. Further, it is recognized that these people most often do not suffer from significant alcohol or drug problems, if any. However, equally, there are some people who have been arrested and charged with driving under the influence who do suffer from alcohol or drug problems. If you are reading this and believe you are one of these unfortunate people please seek help. There are many helpful organizations that were founded to help those people in need of assistance. These organizations will accept you with no questions asked and try to help you. Please contact them and seek help immediately. You deserve a second chance and so does your family. Below is a listing of the group of "anonymous" organizations. They are a great place to start.

FOR HELP WITH POSSIBLE ADDICTION PROBLEMS:

- Alcoholics Anonymous: www.aa.org
- Narcotics Anonymous: www.na.org
- Al-Anon/Alateen: www.al-anon.alateen.org/
- Cocaine Anonymous: www.ca.org
- Marijuana Anonymous: http://www.marijuana-anonymous.org/
- Crystal Meth Anonymous: http://www.crystalmeth.org/

The Michigan Alcohol Screen Test (MAST)

The MAST Test is a simple, self scoring test that helps assess if you have a drinking problem. Please answer YES or NO to the following questions

1. Do you feel you are a normal drinker? ("normal" - drink as much or less than most other people) YES or NO

2. Have you ever awakened the morning after some drinking the night before and found that you could not remember a part of the evening? YES or NO

3. Does any near relative or close friend ever worry or complain about your drinking? YES or NO

4. Can you stop drinking without difficulty after one or two drinks? YES or NO

5. Do you ever feel guilty about your drinking? YES or NO

6. Have you ever attended a meeting of Alcoholics Anonymous (AA)? YES or NO

7. Have you ever gotten into physical fights when drinking? YES or NO

8. Has drinking ever created problems between you and a near relative or close friend? YES or NO

9. Has any family member or close friend gone to anyone for help about your drinking? YES or NO

10. Have you ever lost friends because of your drinking? YES or NO

11. Have you ever gotten into trouble at work because of drinking? YES or NO

12. Have you ever lost a job because of drinking? YES or NO

13. Have you ever neglected your obligations, your family, or your work for two or more days in a row because you were drinking? YES or NO

14. Do you drink before noon fairly often? YES or NO

15. Have you ever been told you have liver trouble such as cirrhosis? YES or NO

16. After heavy drinking have you ever had delirium tremens (D.T.'s), severe shaking, visual or auditory (hearing) hallucinations? YES or NO

17. Have you ever gone to anyone for help about your drinking? YES or NO

18. Have you ever been hospitalized because of drinking? YES or NO

19. Has your drinking ever resulted in your being hospitalized in a psychiatric ward? YES or NO

20. Have you ever gone to any doctor, social worker, clergyman or mental health clinic for help with any emotional problem in which drinking was part of the problem? YES or NO

21. Have you been arrested more than once for driving under the influence of alcohol? YES or NO

22. Have you ever been arrested, even for a few hours because of other behavior while drinking? (If Yes, how many times _____) YES or NO

Scoring

Please score one point if you answered the following:

1. No
2. Yes
3. Yes
4. No
5. Yes
6. Yes
7 through 22: Yes

Add up the scores and compare to the following score card:

0 - 2 No apparent problem
3 - 5 Early or middle problem drinker
6 or more Problem drinker

The Drug Abuse Screening Test (DAST)

Directions: The following questions concern information about your involvement with drugs. Drug abuse refers to (1) the use of prescribed or "over-the-counter" drugs in excess of the directions, and (2) any non-medical use of drugs. Consider the past year (12 months) and carefully read each statement. Then decide whether your answer is YES or NO and check the appropriate space. Please be sure to answer every question.

1. Have you used drugs other than those required for medical reasons? YES / NO

2. Have you abused prescription drugs? YES / NO

3. Do you abuse more than one drug at a time? YES / NO

4. Can you get through the week without using drugs (other than those required for medical reasons)? YES / NO

5. Are you always able to stop using drugs when you want to? YES / NO

6. Do you abuse drugs on a continuous basis? YES / NO

7. Do you try to limit your drug use to certain situations? 8. Have you had "blackouts" or "flashbacks" as a result of drug use? YES / NO

8. Do you ever feel bad about your drug abuse? YES / NO

9. Does your spouse (or parents) ever complain about your involvement with drugs? YES / NO

10. Do your friends or relatives know or suspect you abuse drugs? YES / NO

11. Has drug abuse ever created problems between you and your spouse? YES / NO

12. Has any family member ever sought help for problems related to your drug use? YES / NO

13. Have you ever lost friends because of your use of drugs? YES / NO

14. Have you ever neglected your family or missed work because of your use of drugs? YES / NO

15. Have you ever been in trouble at work because of drug abuse? YES / NO

16. Have you ever lost a job because of drug abuse? YES / NO

17. Have you gotten into fights when under the influence of drugs? YES / NO

18. Have you ever been arrested because of unusual behavior while under the influence of drugs? YES / NO

19. Have you ever been arrested for driving while under the influence of drugs? YES / NO

20. Have you engaged in illegal activities in order to obtain drug? YES / NO

21. Have you ever been arrested for possession of illegal drugs? YES / NO

22. Have you ever experienced withdrawal symptoms as a result of heavy drug intake? YES / NO

23. Have you had medical problems as a result of your drug use (e.g., memory loss, hepatitis, convulsions, bleeding, etc.)? YES / NO

24. Have you ever gone to anyone for help for a drug problem? YES / NO

25. Have you ever been in a hospital for medical problems

related to your drug use? YES / NO

26. Have you ever been involved in a treatment program specifically related to drug use? YES / NO

27. Have you been treated as an outpatient for problems related to drug abuse? YES / NO

Scoring and interpretation: A score of "1" is given for each YES response, except for items 4,5, and 7, for which a NO response is given a score of "1." Based on data from a heterogeneous psychiatric patient population, cutoff scores of 6 through 11 are considered to be optimal for screening for substance use disorders. Using a cutoff score of 6 has been found to provide excellent sensitivity for identifying patients with substance use disorders as well as satisfactory specificity (i.e., identification of patients who do not have substance use disorders). Using a cutoff score of <11 somewhat reduces the sensitivity for identifying patients with substance use disorders, but more accurately identifies the patients who do not have a substance use disorders. Over 12 is definitely a substance abuse problem. In a heterogeneous psychiatric patient population, most items have been shown to correlate at least moderately well with the total scale scores. The items that correlate poorly with the total scale scores appear to be items 4,7,16,20, and 22.

CHAPTER 7

Department of Licensing/Motor Vehicles

If you have been arrested for a DUI it is likely that the officer punched a hole in your license. At that point in time you are on notice that the Department of Licensing (DOL)/ Department of Motor Vehicles (DMV) intends to suspend your license just for being arrested on suspicion of DUI. It does not even matter to the DOL that you might eventually be acquitted of the DUI charge or that the DUI charge might be amended to a lesser offense that does not result in a license suspension. If your breath test result is .08 or higher or if you refused to take the breath test, the arresting officer will report you to the DOL.

However, you should not simply let your license be suspended without a fight. You can challenge the suspension or revocation of your license by returning the Hearing Request to the DOL within a prescribed time period.

If you decide to take no action or miss the deadline the DOL will suspend or revoke your license. This result will not change even if you have valid legal defenses and even if you are found innocent of the DUI charge.

If your license is suspended you must then file proof of

financial responsibility (high risk insurance, also known as SR-22 insurance) for the next three years, the same as if you had been convicted of the DUI charge.

If you have the hearing and lose based on a decision by a Department of Licensing hearing officer, you may appeal the decision within 30 days of the date of the decision. If you do this in Washington State, for instance, it may void your ability to successfully be granted an Ignition Interlock License, so be careful.

In addition to fighting the potential suspension of your license, the DOL hearing has another potential benefit – evidence gathering. Your attorney has an opportunity to subpoena the arresting officer (or other officers involved) and question him/her regarding the details of your case. This "free deposition" may prove insightful and prepare your attorney for trial, negotiation or lead to new legal defense issues that were otherwise unknown. Do not overlook the value of the Department of Licensing hearings.

Finally, if you do lose the DOL Hearing and have your license suspended your home state may offer a "restrictive license" so that you can drive while your regular license is suspended. Check with your attorney for specific information on your state's restrictive license options.

License Suspensions

One of the many collateral consequences of being arrested for DUI is the dreaded, harmful, inconvenient and expensive driver's license suspension. Certain studies have concluded that laws permitting administrative license suspension (ALS) at the time of an arrest for DUI have been found to reduce both alcohol-related fatality accidents and repeat

DUI offenses. Voas, R.B., Tippets, A.S., and Fell, J. *The relationship of alcohol safety laws to drinking drivers in fatal crashes.* Accid Anal Prev 32:483-492 (2000); Voas, R.B., Tippetts, A.S., and Taylor, E.P. *Impact of Ohio administrative license suspension. In:* 42nd Annual Proceedings: Association for the Advancement of Automotive Medicine. Des Plaines, IL: AAAM. (1998) A study of an Ohio ALS law found that first-time and repeat DUI offenders who had their licenses immediately confiscated had significantly lower rates of DUI offenses, moving violations, and crashes during the following two years compared with DUI offenders convicted before the ALS law went into effect. *Id.* Although research shows that license suspensions reduce repeat DUI offenses, there is also evidence that up to 75 percent of suspended drivers continue to drive. Currently 41 states have administrative license suspension laws and only Kentucky, Michigan, Montana, New Jersey, New York, Pennsylvania, Rhode Island, South Dakota, and Tennessee do not

A license suspension received in one state may then be entered into a database called the U.S. Interstate Drivers License Compact. The Drivers License Compact is an agreement between 45 participating states to share information about drivers and their Department of Licensing (DOL/DMV) records that include, but are not limited to, infractions, convictions, driver's license suspensions, license restrictions, revocations, DUI charges, accidents, and eligibility for license reinstatement. Jolly, David N. *The DUI Handbook For The Accused.* Outskirts Press (2007) This information is provided to the National Driver Register (NDR). Both the Drivers License Compact and the Non-Resident Violator Compact are in the process of being merged into one database titled the National Driver Register. *Id.* The main purpose of the NDR database is to share information on drivers who have committed a serious infraction or violation in a state other than where they are licensed to drive. The five states that are not currently members and do not participate in sharing DUI and licensing record information are Georgia, Massachusetts, Michigan, Tennessee and Wisconsin.

Department of Licensing Hearing

At the Department of Licensing hearing, a Hearing Examiner (employed by the DOL!) will determine whether there was 1) a valid stop/contact by the officer, 2) if there was probable cause to arrest, 3) if the petitioner was properly advised of his/her implied consent warnings, and 4) if the breath or blood test was properly administered and the results were 0.08 or above or if the refusal was proper.

The hearing is conducted by a telephone call to the petitioner's attorney's office and the petitioner can attend if he/she wishes (we advise that you do). The hearing officer records the hearing stating the issues to be determined and moves to admit the state's exhibits, namely the police and toxicology report (if it is applicable). The petitioner may also submit exhibits. Once the preliminary matters are dealt with live testimony is elicited as either the Officer or the Petitioner, or both, may testify at the hearing. Typically there is no decision rendered on the day of the hearing and a written decision is mailed to the petitioner and his/her attorney in the weeks following the hearing.

The following information is from attorney Linda Callahan's excellent book *Washington DUI Practice Manual*. The author included a valuable list of reasons the Washington Department of Licensing dismisses cases, although from experience I can inform the reader that these issues and their success depends largely on who the hearing officer is because God did not create them all equally. Regardless, the list below was obtained pursuant to a public disclosure request of the Department of Licensing and has proven valuable at times. Obviously every State has different guidelines but this should serve well as a general guide in all States of the Union. Callahan, Linda M. *Washington DUI Practice Manual: Including Related Driving Offenses*. Washington Practice Series: Volume 32. Thomson West (2008).

Main DOL Checkboxes

Sworn report only
Incomplete defective report
Illegible
Boxes not checked or typos
Missing pages
Officer error
Collateral estoppels
DOL error
Credibility problem
Legal issue
No cause for stop
No probable cause for arrest

Additional DOL Checkboxes

Refusal Issues

Refusal with no actual evidence that petitioner refused
No evidence of refusal, only physical incapacity
Medical evidence showed incapable of providing sample

Refusal suppressed – collateral estoppels

Not given reasonable opportunity to make a BAC decision – collateral estoppels

Not told PBT not alternative to evidentiary test, knowing and intelligent decision – collateral estoppels

Mouth Check Observations issues

Tongue ring – officer failed to comply with WAC 448-16-040

Second mouth check made after first sample with no explanation

No evidence of second mouth check prior to second 15 minute observation period

Invalid sample without new mouth check

Improper waiting period for second sample

Video showed chewing tobacco in mouth, so no 15 minute observation

No evidence that foreign substance found in mouth was ever removed

No evidence of compliance with mouth check and observation period requirements

No evidence of uneventful observation period

No evidence person did not vomit during observation period

Insufficient evidence officer observed during whole observation period

Observation boxes not checked by officer and missing narrative pages

Foreign substance in mouth

No indication of what the foreign substance removed from mouth was

Box not checked regarding foreign substance in mouth

Mouth check less than fifteen minutes before BAC sample

Mouth check time was prior to driving

Wrong time for observation period keyed into the breath ticket

BAC Machine or Operator Issues

QAP not current

QAP signed but not dated next to signature

Insufficient thermometer

No evidence BAC operator certified no BAC permit card

BAC permit card expired

No BAC evidence

No BAC – collateral estoppels

No BAC ticket

Error in solution change – tech not current in certification

BAC ticket not legible – data missing on database

BAC ticket not legible

BAC Certification box not checked, narrative silent, no BAC card

Officer stated thermometer 34.9 degrees (thermometer range only 33.5-34.5)

Simulator Temperature not within 33.7-34.3 Degree Range

Error codes not addressed in narrative

Repeated DataMaster ambient failure

Blood Test Issues

Insufficient evidence of reasonable suspicion under influence of drugs

Insufficient evidence of lawful blood draw

Trooper reported blood test results prior to analysis

Report of alcohol by analysis was dated after Trooper reported it

Illegible blood toxicology report

No blood toxicology report, sworn signed prior to results being known

No authority to request blood draw because BAC inoperable

ICW Issues

ICW's read after breath test administered according to timeline

ICW's modified crossing phrases out – unsworn narrative (insufficient evidence – ICW issues)

No evidence ICWs were provided in Spanish – all other paper work was Spanish interpreted

Insufficient evidence of contents of Spanish ICW warnings played off CD to petitioner

Not properly apprised of the ICWs

ICW confusion

No evidence of ICWs being given

Confusion of ICWs was not clarified

Confusion expressed – then misled by attempted clarification

ICW warning defective

ICW misleading – collateral estoppel under 21 issue

ICW misleading – collateral estoppels

Outdated ICW warnings given to driver

ICWs for blood not given

Cause for Initial Stop Issues

Initial contact based on citizen complaint w/no sworn statement as referenced by the officer

Insufficient evidence of impairment

Campbell v. DOL problem – insufficient independent basis for stop

Witness evidence for No PC to stop. Trooper failed to appear

No PC to initial stop

No PC to initial stop – dim license plate bulb

No PC to initial stop – RCW 46.61.210 requires lights & siren for emergency

No PC to initial stop – no jurisdiction

No PC to initial stop – no evidence re: speed violation

No PC to initial stop – evidence of wrong speed limit used by officer

No PC to initial stop – only touched lane lines, no crossing

No PC to initial stop – officer never established need to dim headlights

No PC to initial stop – no need to signal leaving private complex, little driving

No PC to initial stop – officer never listed how they established speed violation

No PC to initial stop – collateral estoppel

No PC to initial stop – no narrative report received by DOL

No PC to initial stop – no report from officer who stopped person

No PC to initial stop – pre-textual stop

PC for Arrest Issues

No PC for arrest

No PC for arrest – vehicle on private property

No PC for arrest – driver turns off car and leaves then no

driving (*Sunnyside v. Wendt*)
No evidence petitioner was driving
Time of arrest preceded time for PC to arrest
Compelled FSTs – insufficient PC to arrest
Officer had no proof of training/certification to perform
    HGN or PBT training
Box not checked for PBT protocol

DOL Errors

No ten days notice for hearing
Notice of hearing not sent to petitioner or counsel
DOL error in scheduling hearing – double booked
DOL error in scheduling hearing – after sixtieth day
No discovery sent out

Officer Errors

Officer subpoenaed and failed to appear (*Lytle v. DOL*)
Police report written entirely by one officer but submitted
    by another
Details of report not geographically possible
Officer failed to mark authority to arrest box
Officer did not sign report
Officer did not sign and date report
No narrative submitted
Officer did not swear to report (failed to comply with
    9A.72.085)
Narrative report post dated beyond certification page 1 of
    exhibit 1 (9A.72.085)
Officer did not submit report to DOL within 72 hours as
    required in 46.20.308(5)(e)
Officer certified report prior to BrAC results, WSP Tech

retrieved BrAC ticket later

Officer failed to prepare for testimony, thwarting effect cross-examination

Officer could not recall events

Officer called for petitioner's additional blood test at jail and jail would not let them in

Restricted Licenses

Most states offer the driver an option to drive if their license is suspended. This option in called a "restricted license." The names of these licenses differ from state to state and the rules for each of these licenses similarly differ. It is important to check with an attorney in your specific state or the local DOL/DMV. Usually the DOL/DMV has a website that provides some limited information on these licenses. Be certain to consult with an attorney regarding your restrictive license options as you may not be eligible for all options.

Commercial Drivers

Governing the Commercial Driver and the privilege to drive is the Commercial Motor Vehicle Safety Act of 1986. The Act continued to give states the right to issue CDLs, but the federal government established minimum requirements that must be met when issuing a CDL.

For those with a Commercial Driver's License (CDL) and who are stopped for a DUI the consequences of a license suspension can be particularly troublesome. Matters become worse if the holder of the CDL is stopped (and arrested) for DUI while driving a commercial vehicle. When a police officer determines that a commercial driver has any alcohol in his system while driving, the driver will immediately be issued an out of service order valid for twenty four hours which means the driver may not operate any commercial vehicle for a twenty four hour period. The officer may then require the driver to submit to a test of his breath to determine the alcohol content. If the driver has an alcohol concentration of .04 or more, or if the driver refuses to submit to a breath test, the officer will submit a sworn statement reporting these findings to the DOL within 72 hours of the incident.

Once the DOL has received this report and notified the driver, the driver may request a hearing within 30 days. If no hearing was requested or if it is proven at the hearing that the driver had an alcohol concentration of .04 or more, or refused the breath test, the driver will be suspended from driving a commercial vehicle. For a first violation, the driver will be suspended for one year and for a second or subsequent violation the driver will be suspended for life.

Like a regular driver, even if the commercial driver wins the DOL hearing and defeats the administrative suspension, he or she still faces suspensions if convicted of a DUI in the criminal court. In summary, if you are a CDL holder you must be very careful in how you proceed with your DUI. Simply because the DUI is amended to a lesser charge may not have any benefit to your CDL.

Agreements and Compacts between States

There are many different agreements and compacts that the Department of Licensing offices in different states use to exchange information. In the context of this book and DUI law, some are more important than others. The most important is the Driver License Compact and as such this will be discussed in some detail. However, here is a brief overview of the agreements and compacts that most states are members of and of some relevance in the DUI context:

- *Driver License Compact* – not every state participates but those who do voluntarily contribute information to the National Driving Register (NDR) regarding driver license suspensions and revocations.
- *Non-Resident Violator Compact* – similar to the Driver License Compact, not all states participate, but those who do send information (including all traffic offenses) back to your home state.
- *Driver License Reciprocity (DLR)* - provides electronic exchange of driver history data (not all states participate).
- *Driver License Agreement (DLA)* – only some states participate, it is an effort to provide one driver record instead of having different records in each state.

Drivers License Compact and Non-Resident Violator Compact

The U.S. Interstate Drivers License Compact is an agreement between the 45 participating states to share information about drivers and their Department of Licensing (DOL) records that include, but are not limited to, infractions, convictions, driver's license suspensions, license restrictions, revocations, DUI charges, accidents, and eligibility for license reinstatement. This information is provided to the National Driver Register (NDR).

The Drivers License Compact is an agreement between states to consider only one driving record per driver, and that record will follow the licensee from state to state, rather than a new record being created if an out of state license is issued.

Both the Drivers License Compact and the Nonresident Violator Compact Member states communicate with each other if a licensee of one state receives a ticket in another state.

Both the Drivers License Compact and the Non-Resident Violator Compact are in the process of being merged into one database titled the National Driver Register. The main purpose of the NDR database is to share information on drivers who have committed a serious infraction or violation in a state other than where they are licensed to drive. The DOL of each member state checks the NDR each time a person applies for a driver's license.

All States are members of the Drivers License Compact except for Georgia, Michigan, Wisconsin, Tennessee (dropped out in 1997). Nevada repealed the authorizing legislation in 2007, though it still generally conforms to the agreement through regulations.

All States are members of the Non-Resident Violator Compact except Alaska, California, Michigan, Montana, Oregon, and Wisconsin.

The National Driver Register (NDR)

The National Driver Register (NDR) is a computerized database of information about drivers who have had their licenses revoked or suspended, or who have been convicted of serious traffic violations such as driving while impaired by alcohol or drugs.

When a person applies, either as a new applicant or as a renewal, for a driver's license the state DOL/DMV must check to see if the name is on the NDR Problem Driver Pointer

System (PDPS) (as required by federal regulation--see 23 CFR 1327.5(b)(1). If a person has been reported to the NDR by any state as a "problem driver", the prospective licensing state must investigate the driver's history from the state that added the NDR record. Depending on the results of the investigation and the state's own laws, the prospective licensing state may be required to deny the license. Thus, this "PDPS check" enables the state MVAs to prevent someone with a suspended or revoked driver's license in one state from obtaining a driver's license in another state. The PDPS check also makes it harder for a person to obtain more than one driver's license at any one time.

State motor vehicle agencies provide NDR with the names of individuals who have lost their privilege or who have been convicted of a serious traffic violation. When a person applies for a driver's license the state checks to see if the name is on the NDR file. If a person has been reported to the NDR as a problem driver, the license may be denied. For specific information, or to apply for a copy of your own record on file with the NDR, log on to the following website: http://www.nationaldriverregister.com

The following individuals, businesses, and agencies are authorized to received information from the NDR:

- Any individual under the provisions of the Privacy Act.
- State and federal driver's license officials.
- Current or prospective employers of motor vehicles operators.
- Air Carriers for Pilot Applicants.
- The Federal Railroad Administration and employers of railroad engineers.

- The Federal Aviation Administration for airmen medical certification.
- The U.S. Coast Guard for merchant marine certification.
- The National Transportation Safety Board.
- Federal Highway Administration for Accident Investigations.

CHAPTER **8**

DUI Defenses And Avoiding A (Another) DUI

DUI Defenses

There are many potential defenses that can be raised in a DUI case. Every good DUI attorney will be consistently on the forefront of changes and challenges to the DUI statutes, police practices, and the constitutionality of DUI procedures. Unless your attorney practices DUI cases on a regular basis he may not be familiar with recent changes as this area of the law is constantly evolving. While there are certainly more defenses than are listed below, these are the most common defenses available in the average DUI case. If you have a good DUI attorney he should be able to draw on his experience and expertise and be creative when constructing a defense on your behalf.

How to Beat a DUI

360 Legal Defenses and Arguments

Driving

Lack of probable cause to stop and/or contact the vehicle

Weaving inside the lane is not illegal

Driving over the fog line once may not validate the stop and/or contact of the vehicle

Anonymous report of DUI – officer must corroborate the report

Corpus Delicti – must prove defendant was actually driving

Safely Off the Roadway – a defense to "physical control"

Videos in Patrol Car – may contradict officer's report

Observations of Driver -Physical Appearance

Clothing and Grooming

Is there an innocent explanation for the defendant's disheveled clothing?

Why had the defendant not shaved or combed his hair?

Are there any other witnesses to the defendant's appearance within an hour of the arrest?

Can the officer's conclusions be used to discredit other testimony?

Eyes

Does the defendant suffer from an eye disorder?

Is the normal appearance of defendant's eyes red, glassy, watery, or bloodshot?

Was the defendant suffering from fatigue, lack of sleep, or eye strain?

Was there significant air pollution on the day of the arrest?

If a pupil reaction test was given:

-Was the officer qualified to administer the test and render medical conclusions?

-How were size of pupils and speed of their reaction measured?

-Is the officer familiar with nonalcoholic causes of slow pupil reaction?

Flushed Face

Is the defendant's facial complexion normally flushed or red?

Was the defendant nervous, angry, or otherwise emotionally upset at the time of the officer's observations?

Are there causes for a flushed appearance other than alcohol?

Breath Odor

As alcohol has little or no odor, was the officer smelling an unusually strong beverage flavoring such as that of beer or wine?

Does the officer contend that he can tell what the defendant was drinking, when, and how much?

Does or did the defendant simply have bad breath or acetone (caused by diabetes)?

Was the defendant belching prior to the officer smelling his breath?

Did the presence of an odor of alcohol have an instrumental effect in the forming of the officer's opinion of intoxication?

Was the defendant's last drink within one hour of driving?

Speech

Was the officer familiar with the defendant's normal speech prior to the arrest?

Does the defendant normally speak in a thick, slurred, stuttering, and/or confused manner?

Did nervousness, anger, or embarrassment affect the defendant's speech?

Are there any other witnesses to the defendant's speech characteristics within an hour of the arrest?

Did the police report permit any alternatives to slurred speech, such as "good," "fair," "repetitive," and "fast?"

Was the officer able to understand the defendant's answers to the numerous questions?

Does the defendant have an accent?

Is English the defendant's native language?

Do any audio or video tapes exist?

Field Sobriety Tests (FSTs)

Initial Considerations

Did the tests consist of the federally recommended "standardized" battery of tests: walk-and-turn, one-leg stand, and horizontal nystagmus?

-If so, were they administered and scored as recommended?

-If not, why were tests not approved by NHTSA used by the officer?

Can the FSTs be suppressed at a motion hearing?

Should the officer and prosecutor be instructed to refrain from using such terms as "test" or "fail"?

When was the officer trained in FSTs?

Has the officer received refresher courses in FSTs?

Has the officer received ARIDE training?
Is the officer an instructor for FSTs?

Defendant's Condition

Was the defendant 50 pounds or more overweight?
Was the defendant 65 years of age or older?
Was the defendant suffering from any illness affecting his balance or coordination?
Was the defendant taking any drugs or medication that might affect his balance?
Did the defendant have any physical disabilities affecting his ability to take the tests?
Was the defendant upset by or injured in a traffic collision?
Was the defendant suffering from any emotional reactions to the procedure - fear, embarrassment, anger, nervousness?
Was the defendant wearing shoes with high heels while performing the tests?

Administration of Field Sobriety Tests

Were the tests given on a smooth and level area?
Was the area covered with gravel, loose dirt, or other possible obstructions?
Were the tests administered near passing vehicles, creating nose and wind waves?
Did the lighting conditions impede the defendant's successful performance?
Did the weather conditions make the tests more difficult to perform?
Did the police vehicle have flashing lights creating a strobe effect?

Could unclear instructions by the officer have contributed to test results?

Was the defendant given the opportunity to practice each of the tests once before attempting them? Why not?

What was the physical line used in the walk-the-line test?

Did he demonstrate to the defendant by first performing each test?

Does "passing" involve a subjective opinion by the officer?

Had the officer already formed an opinion that the defendant was intoxicated?

Are there any objective criteria?

Did the officer use negative scoring?

Did the officer take into consideration the "impaired learning curve" (fear, nervousness) in assessing pass/fail?

Corroboration

Were any videotapes or photographs taken of the defendant performing the tests?

Were any audio or video devices available to the officer, if so, and they were not used, why not?

Are there any defense witnesses who observed the tests being given?

Were any potential witnesses prevented by the police from viewing the tests?

Did the officer diagram the walk-the-line and/or finger-to-nose tests as they were performed?

Was he capable of recalling all details when he later drafted his report?

Can a comparison of the defendant's signature and/or

handwriting be effectively made?

Horizontal Gaze Nystagmus (HGN)

Admissibility
Is evidence of the HGN test admissible at trial?
If so, is it available to prove consumption of alcohol only (not impairment)?
Is the officer qualified as an expert?
Does the test pass the state and/or *Frye* standards?
Does the evidence consist of testimony as to the indicated blood-alcohol level, or as to whether the defendant passed or failed?

Foundation
Was the officer qualified to administer the HGN test?
Has he had sufficient training and experience?
Is he familiar with the physiological theory behind the test?
Is the officer aware of the many sources for error inherent in the test?

Administration
Was the test administered according to the standardized procedures?
Did the officer ask the defendant if he was wearing contacts and note the answer?
Did the officer have the defendant remove glasses before testing?
Did the officer tell the defendant, "I am going to check your eyes"?
Did the officer instruct the defendant: "Keep your head

still and follow this stimulus with your eyes only"?

Was the defendant told: "Keep focusing on this stimulus until I tell you to stop"?

Did the officer hold the stimulus 12 to 15 inches from the defendant's nose and slightly above eye level?

Pupils not equal in size may indicate a head injury; did the officer check to see if the defendant's pupils were equal in size?

Eyes that don't track together could indicate a possible medical disorder, injury, or blindness; did the officer check the defendant's eyes for the ability to track together?

Did the officer move the stimulus smoothly?

Did the officer move the stimulus two seconds out, two seconds back, for each eye?

Was the stimulus moved to maximum deviation, and held for four seconds for each eye?

Did the officer check to see if the onset of nystagmus occurred before 45 degrees?

Was the sclera (white of the eye) visible?

Did the officer check for each clue at least twice in each eye?

Was the defendant facing away from flashing lights?

Did the defendant exhibit the standardized clues?

-Lack of smooth pursuit

-Distinct nystagmus at maximum deviation

-Onset of nystagmus prior to 45 degrees

-Did the defendant exhibit other clues?

-Did the defendant sway noticeably during the test?

-Did the defendant keep his head still during the test?

Does this testimony conflict with the officer's earlier or later testimony that the defendant was staggering, weaving, or unstable on his feet?

Sources of Error

Was the angle of onset measured accurately and honestly?

Was the angle of onset measured with a template, or by estimate?

Has the officer received training in estimating angles?

Has the officer undergone recent verification of his ability to estimate angles?

Did the officer simply use the defendant's shoulders to measure 45 degrees?

Was the jerking of the eye observed by the officer due to his moving the focal object in a jerking manner?

Is there any evidence corroborative of the officer's testimony concerning the angle?

Did the officer use the objective scoring system recommended by the NHTSA?

Are there any sources of possible error in the test?

Is the officer aware of physiological grounds for error?

Had the defendant consumed coffee, smoked a cigarette, or taken an aspirin?

Did the defendant suffer from any physiological problems that would affect nystagmus, such as influenza, streptococcus, vertigo, or epilepsy?

Is the defendant hypertensive or hypotensive?

Was the defendant carsick?

Were there any inner ear problems?

Was the defendant suffering from eyestrain or eye muscle fatigue?

Is the officer aware of the effects of circadian rhythm on the onset of nystagmus?

Walk-and-Turn

Was the test administered in accordance with the standardized procedures?

Were the required conditions for the administration of this test met?

Was the test conducted on a dry, hard, level, non-slippery surface?

Was there a designated straight line?

Was the test administered under relatively safe conditions?

Were the proper instructions given?

Did the officer tell the defendant: "Place your left foot on the line"?

Did the officer further explain: "Place your right foot on the line ahead of the left foot, with the heel of your right foot against the toe of your left foot"?

Was the defendant told: "Place your arms down at your side"?

Was the defendant instructed: "Keep this position until I tell you to begin; do not start to walk until I tell you to do so"?

Did the officer verify that the defendant understood the stance was to be maintained while instructions were given?

If the defendant lapsed from the stance during the instructions, did the officer cease instructions until the stance was resumed?

Did the officer tell the defendant that he would be required to do nine heel-to-toe steps down the line, turn around, and take nine heel-to-toe steps up the line?

Did the officer demonstrate several heel-to-toe steps?

Did the officer demonstrate the turn?

Did the officer tell the defendant to look at his feet, keep arms at sides, count steps aloud, and not to stop walking until the test is completed?

Did the officer ask the defendant whether he understood and re-explain what was not understood?

Were the proper procedures followed while the defendant performed the test?

Was the defendant told to begin?

If the defendant staggered or stopped, did the officer allow him to resume from the point of interruption rather than go back to the beginning?

The officer should not have followed alongside the defendant.

The officer should not have been within three or four feet of the defendant during the test.

Did the defendant exhibit any of the standardized clues?

-Lose balance during instructions (feet must break apart from the heel-to-toe stance);

-Start walking too soon;

-Stop while walking to steady self;

-Miss heel-to-toe while walking (by 1/2 inch or more);

-Raise arms from side while walking (6 inches or more);

-Step off the line;

-Turn improperly;

-Take wrong number of steps.

One-Leg-Stand

Was the test administered according to the standardized procedures?

Were the required conditions for the administration of the test met?

Was the test administered on a smooth, level surface?

Was the lighting adequate?

Were the proper instructions given?

Was the defendant told to stand with feet together and arms at sides?

Did the officer tell the defendant not to start until told to do so?

Did the officer ask the defendant if he understood?

Was the defendant told to stand on either foot with the other foot held straight and about six inches off the ground, toes pointed out?

Did the officer demonstrate the proper stance?

Did the officer instruct the subject to count from 1 to 30 by thousands until told to stop?

Did the officer demonstrate the count for several seconds?

Did the officer ask the defendant if he understood, and if not, did the officer re-explain? Were the proper procedures followed while the defendant performed the test?

Did the officer tell the defendant to begin?

If the defendant stopped or put his foot down, did the officer allow him or her to begin at the point of interruption?

Was the defendant permitted to remove his shoes?

The officer should not stand within three feet of the suspect during the test.

The officer should not move around during the test.

Did the defendant exhibit any of the standardized clues?

-Sway in trying to balance;

-Put foot down;

-Hop;

-Raise arm from side 6 inches or more.

Preliminary Breath Test (PBT)

Was the device approved by State Statute?

Did the officer advise the subject prior to the test that the PBT was voluntary?

Did the operator perform the test according to the policies and procedures approved by the state toxicologist?

Did the operator perform the following test protocol?

-The operator shall advise the subject that this is a voluntary test, and that it is not an alternative to any evidential breath alcohol test;

- The operator shall determine by observation or inquiry, that the subject has not consumed any alcohol in the fifteen minutes prior to administering the test. If the subject has consumed alcohol during that period, the officer should not administer the screening test for probable cause purposes until fifteen minutes have passed. If the subject responds that they have not consumed any alcohol in the last fifteen minutes, the officer may offer the subject the opportunity to provide a breath sample into the PBT;

-Ensure a blank test result is obtained;

-Have the subject exhale into the mouthpiece with a

full and continuous exhalation;
-Observe the results.

Breath Tests

Breath Analysis
Was the machine properly certified and maintained?
Was the operator properly trained and certified?
Was the machine accurately calibrated?
Was the simulator solution mixed correctly?
Could the alcohol in the solution have become depleted?
What was the temperature of the solution?
Could there have been leakage in the vapor tube?
Could radio frequency interference (RFI) have affected the reading?
What possible sources of RFI existed in the breath machine's environment?
Does the machine use infrared spectroscopy?
Is it specific for ethyl alcohol?
What compounds found on the human breath will it detect as "alcohol"?
Does the machine have an acetone detector? If yes, was it working properly? If no, why not?
Does the machine have an acetaldehyde detector? If yes, was it working properly? If no, why not?
Is the client a diabetic or has he been fasting?
What compounds containing the methyl group has he ingested or been exposed to?
Could the breath test have been conducted during the client's absorptive phase?
Had the client recently eaten food before drinking?
Was mouth alcohol present?

Did the client burp, belch, hiccup, or regurgitate within 15 minutes of the breath test?

Did he consume any alcohol within 15 minutes of the test?

Did he observe the client constantly for 15 minutes before administering the test?

Could the operator have manipulated the observation period times (the officer manually types in the beginning of the observation period)?

Were there any other people in the BAC room/area during the observation period that could have been distractions to the officer?

Does he wear dentures, use dental adhesive, or have dental caps that could trap alcohol?

Did he use any mouthwash, cough syrup, throat spray, breath freshener, or other product containing alcohol?

What was the client's body temperature at the time of the test?

Could the client's breathing pattern have affected the breath test?

Could stress have had an effect on the test?

Was a sterile new mouthpiece for both breath tests used?

Was the machine purged with room air containing alcohol vapor from the client or previously tested suspects?

Do the machine's records indicate any failures or mechanical problems before or since the test?

Has the machine been modified in any way affecting its status as a state-approved device?

Is operator/officer familiar with the theory and operation of the BAC machine in use?

Did he follow the manufacturer's checklist? Can he recall each step?

Is the machine specific for alcohol?
What other compounds found on the breath will be reported as alcohol by the machine?
Could the client have had acetaldehyde in his system? Acetone? Ketones? Paint or glue fumes? Other compounds?
Was there any source of radio frequency interference in the area of the machine when the client was tested?
Any police transmitters? Walkie-talkies? Televisions? Electric door locks? Microwave ovens? Police car transmitters in the parking lot? Teletype machines? Computers? Radios? Fluorescent lighting?
Could the machine have been affected by a mechanical or electrical problem, such as a drop in line voltage?
How many malfunctions are recognized as possible by the manufacturer?
Are all of these detected by the machine's internal computer?
Would a defect in the computer or its software be detectable?
Were all operating temperatures as required by the manufacturer?
Could condensation have formed in the breath tube as a result of being operated at an improper temperature?
Were there any possible problems with the machine's temperature, humidity, optics, or age?
Was a self-checking diagnostic system available in the BAC machine?
Was it run immediately before or after the client's test? Why not?
Are there any generic problems with breath testing?

Can the prosecution establish that the client's partition ratio was 2100:1?

Blood Draws

Blood Analysis

Was the laboratory conducting the analysis properly licensed?

Was the individual drawing the blood sample qualified and/or licensed?

Was the laboratory technician who analyzed the sample properly licensed?

Was the equipment calibrated accurately?

Was the syringe used to withdraw the sample sterilized?

Was the arm swabbed with alcohol or any other substance that could contaminate the sample?

Did the blood sample come from the client's artery or vein?

Is there a regulation as to which must be used?

Would an arterial sample give a falsely high BAC?

Would a venous sample give a falsely high BAC?

Was the blood sample refrigerated at all times?

Was the proper preservative added and in the correct amount?

Could sodium fluoride have caused a higher BAC because of a "salting out" effect?

Was the proper anticoagulant added and in the correct amount?

Was the vial properly sealed, or could evaporation have caused an increased BAC?

Can the prosecution account for the chain of custody of the analyzed sample?

What method of analysis was used?

If gas chromatography was used, were there any sources of radio frequency interference in or near the laboratory?

If the Kozelka-Hines (dichromate) method was used, could acetone, acetalde-hyde, or other substances have caused a false BAC?

Was the sample one of a larger batch of samples analyzed en masse?

Did the analyzed sample consist of whole blood or of serum/plasma?

If serum/plasma, has the laboratory adjusted the BAC downward to allow for the serum/plasma concentration being 15 to 20 percent higher?

If so, did the laboratory use an average conversion ratio? Was that ratio demonstrably applicable to the client's sample?

Is a portion of the blood sample available to counsel for independent analysis?

Urine Tests

Is urinalysis an approved method of blood-alcohol analysis?

Was a more accurate method available?

Were duplicate samples obtained?

Was the laboratory conducting the analysis properly licensed?

Was the laboratory technician who analyzed the sample properly licensed?

Was the equipment accurately calibrated?

Was the sample one of a larger batch of samples analyzed en masse?

How long after the arrest was the sample obtained?

Was the client required to void his bladder 20 minutes before producing a sample?

Did he void incompletely on purpose?

Is it possible to void completely? Did old urine involuntarily left after a "complete" void contaminate the new urine?

Did the urinalysis assume a urine/blood ratio of 1.33:1?

What evidence exists of the client's actual ratio?

What range of possible BACs would be obtained by applying the range of possible urine/blood ratios?

Could the urine sample have been contaminated?

Could the client have had a substance on his hands that could have contaminated the sample urine?

Was the sample jar sterile?

Was the proper preservative added and in the correct amount?

Was the urine sample refrigerated at all times?

Could the presence of Candida albicans in the urine sample have caused the production of alcohol?

Was the vial properly sealed, or could evaporation have caused an increased BAC?

Can the prosecution account for the chain of custody of the analyzed sample?

What method of analysis was used?

If gas chromatography was used, were there any sources of radio frequency interference in or near the laboratory?

If the Kozelka-Hines (dichromate) method was used, could any substances other than alcohol have caused a false BAC?

Is a portion of the urine sample available to counsel for independent analysis?

Medical Defenses

The BAC, field sobriety test performance, or physical observations (that look like intoxication) may be explained by the following diseases or conditions

Does the driver suffer from gastroesophageal reflux disease (GERD)?

Does the driver suffer from diabetes?

Does the driver suffer from chronic obstructive pulmonary disease (COPD)?

Does the driver suffer from post traumatic stress disorder (PTSD)?

Does the driver suffer from Parkinson's disease?

Does the driver suffer from cerebral palsy?

Does the driver suffer from multiple sclerosis?

Does the driver suffer from Ménière's disease?

Does the driver suffer from head injuries or concussions?

Does the driver suffer from foot, leg, or back problems or injuries?

Does the driver suffer from an eye condition?

Legal Defenses

The Stop/Contact

Did the officer have probable cause to stop the client's car?

Are there specific and articulable facts present?

Did probable cause depend at least in part on a tip?

Is the informant known and reliable?

Was the information forwarded by a dispatcher or other source, constituting "double hearsay"?

Is there any risk of a jury hearing evidence of the informant's information?

Detention

Did the officer have probable cause to detain the client for further investigation?
Was the detention unreasonably long in time?

Arrest

Did the officer have probable cause to arrest the client?
Did the officer have legal authority to make an arrest?
Did a lawful arrest precede any blood-alcohol test or interrogation?
Was the evidence used by the officer to determine probable cause to arrest, validly obtained?

Sobriety Checkpoints

(Not legal in Idaho, Iowa, Michigan, Minnesota, Oregon, Rhode Island, Texas, Washington, Wisconsin, and Wyoming)

Did the client's DUI stop result from a roadblock or checkpoint?
Is there a legislatively developed procedure for roadblocks?
Do guidelines exist by statute or case precedent?
Did the roadblock or checkpoint comply with acceptable standards?
Was the decision-making process accomplished at the supervisory level?

Were effective limits placed on the *discretion* of officers at the checkpoint?

Was the checkpoint administered in a *safe manner*?

Was the *location* chosen a reasonable one?

How intrusive were the *time* and *duration* of the checkpoint?

Were sufficient *indicia of authority* clearly visible to the public?

Was the *length of detention* minimal?

Was there sufficient advance *publicity* as to the time, location, and nature of the checkpoint?

What reports, memoranda, notes, etc., are available through discovery?

Was the roadblock valid under the relevant provisions of the state constitution?

Incriminating Statements

Did the client make any incriminating statements?

Was the statement given as a result of custodial interrogation?

If under arrest, was *Miranda* given?

If Miranda was advised, did the defendant waived the right to remain silent?

Is the statement relevant to the issue of intoxication?

Does any probative value outweigh the prejudicial effect?

Is the appropriate procedure for suppression a pre-trial motion, motion in limine, an objection, or a motion out of hearing of the jury?

Refusal to Submit to Chemical Testing

Do the client's words and/or conduct constitute a refusal?
If arguably they do not, does any probative value out-
weigh the prejudicial effect?
Can the refusal be suppressed?
Was the refusal due to consciousness of guilt?
Can the prosecution lay a foundation showing the reason
for the refusal?
Did the client refuse to take field sobriety tests?

Suppressing Blood-Alcohol Evidence

Did the client consent to testing?
Was he advised of the implied consent warnings?
Were these warnings provided in a timely manner prior to
the breath test request?
Did the defendant express confusion after the reading of
the implied consent warnings?
Did the officer read the implied consent warnings ver batum?
Was the consent obtained through coercion?
Is there any independent evidence of the consent?
Did the client have a right to a choice of tests?
Was he advised of this right?
Was the client denied access to counsel before submitting
to a test?
Did the officer check the subject's mouth more than 15
minutes prior to the test (or according to the State
statute)?
If the officer found a foreign substance in the subject's
mouth, was it removed and a new observation time
started?

Was a blood sample obtained through excessive force?
Was the client denied an opportunity to have an indepen-
dent blood-alcohol test?
Did the officer advise him of this right?
Did the officer assist or offer to assist in obtaining the in-
dependent sample?
Can the prosecution establish a sufficient foundation for
the introduction of the blood-alcohol evidence?
Is the blood or urine sample available for re-analysis?

Miscellaneous

What is the reputation of the reporting/arresting officer(s)?
Language Issues: Did the officer get a language inter-
preter for the interpretation of the implied consent
warnings?

Avoiding A (Another) DUI

If you have a drink with friends, colleagues, clients, or
at a sporting event and drive, you are eligible to be stopped
and potentially charged with a DUI. Regardless of whether
you have only one drink or multiple drinks, you are a candidate to be stopped by a police officer if you chose to drive.
I have represented (or prosecuted) too many individuals to
mention who have been charged with a DUI with a blood
alcohol concentration level of less than 0.080. If you once
thought that you were okay to drive with one or two drinks
in your system, you were very wrong.

If you have had a couple of drinks (or a couple too many)
consider these tips:

- Do not drink and drive
- Avoid driving late at night
- Drive a vehicle that is in proper working order
- Do not drive from a bar (drinking establishment) parking lot
- Turn your head lights on at night
- When you see the officer's lights, pull over immediately
- Make a good impression-be polite
- Be prepared to be stopped
- Remain silent, but if you don't, be honest
- If you had "one for the road," tell the officer
- Politely refuse all field sobriety tests (FSTs)
- If you take the FSTs inform the Officer of any physical impairment
- Demand to speak to an attorney at the police station and before the breath test
- Request the Administrative License Hearing within the time limit
- Hire an experienced DUI attorney

CHAPTER 9

The Court, Prosecutor, Judge, and Plea Negotiations

The Court

State District Courts

District Courts generally have elected Judges and elected prosecuting attorneys. As a result these courts tend to be more politically biased than Municipal Courts. As a result of the election process and the required election promises, prosecuting attorneys and Judges may face community or self imposed pressure to be hard on DUI defendants. Most every elected prosecuting attorney has a campaign platform with a mandate of prosecuting more DUI drivers. The elected prosecutors also face the added pressure of feeling as though it is imperative they have the political support of the police at election time.

Municipal Courts

Municipal Courts may have elected Judges or in some

instances, appointed Judges. The appointed Judges are common place in smaller cities or towns. Often these "appointed" Judges are appointed by committee, often comprising the Police Chief, the City Mayor, and possibly the Municipal Court Supervisor. As a result the Judge's audience is not the electorate but the police department (same organization that accuses you of DUI). Sometimes justice is not so blind.

Courtroom Appearance

There was an advertisement in the early 1990's with the tennis player Andre Agassi that proclaimed "Image is Everything." While most of us would disagree with that statement there are times when it has a limited role – such a time is in court. It is vital to present yourself well in court. Clearly this is something that you should discuss with your attorney however there are some basic rules that are relevant in any court room setting.

The court is a business type of environment. Attorneys wear suits and Judges wear robes so you should also dress in your "Sunday best." Dress as if you are going to a job interview. Hence you should be clean and neat, well manicured, well dressed, and dressed conservatively. If you have body piercings remove them or, if possible, hide them. As far as tattoos, the court room setting is not the environment to show off the naked lady tattoo on your arm. Hide it! Shorts, tank tops, hats, sandals and flip-flops are not permitted and do not chew gum or take food or drinks into the court room. Also, turn off your cell phone (many defendants and attorneys have lost their phone to the court as a result of a cell phone that has rung at the wrong time). This should be obvious but based on my years of going to court, it clearly isn't.

The other important thing to remember about the court

room is you must be on time. Judges do not take kindly to tardiness. If you are late to court you are running the risk of receiving a bench-warrant for your troubles. Also, if you are late it puts pressure on your attorney who must explain to the prosecutor and Judge why you are not there. This is not the preferred style of plea negotiating. In summary, be early to court.

Finally, when you address the Judge do so with respect. When you answer a question do so clearly and always address the Judge as "Your Honor." It goes without saying but be pleasant, do not use foul language, and maintain good posture (stand upright and no hands in pockets).

The Prosecuting Attorney

The prosecuting attorney is the key person, besides your attorney, who will determine the outcome of your case. Knowing the prosecuting attorney who will have control of your case can be critical to success or failure. There are some instances in my practice when I am not familiar with an individual prosecutor. This is not unusual as new prosecutor's come and go. However, in situations when I do not know the prosecutor I make sure that I ask fellow defense attorneys or other prosecutors in order to find out more. I need to know the prosecutor's weaknesses and reputation before I start battling him in court. Failing to know the prosecutor is a big mistake.

The Rookie

The Rookie is the prosecutor who has recently graduated from law school or some circumstances, still in law school. Generally, he has less than one year of practice. The rookie is new to the business and is looking for experience. Hence, he is willing to take some cases to trial simply to gather experience and is either willing to overlook serious issues with his case or alternatively cannot see the serious issues with his case due to inexperience. It is these issues that make the rookie dangerous.

Rookies are not necessarily easy to work with. Due to the fact that they have limited experience and have not seen every DUI defense and may not have faced your attorney previously they often do not understand the complexity of DUI cases. Further, these rookie prosecutors are often gung ho and trying to make an impression. Additionally, trying to negotiate with them is often an exercise in futility due to the fact that typically they are given very little discretion and are unable to deviate from the party rule. In cases such as this it is best to go over their heads and talk directly to their supervisor to get the deal your attorney believes is reasonable. Rookies are found in both State district courts and municipal courts.

The Career Prosecutor

The career prosecutor comes in two general forms, those who love the work and feel passionate about it or those who simply don't want to do anything else (don't get these two types confused, they are different). The good news about career prosecutors is that they have seen DUI cases and defenses thousands of times. Your attorney need not bother trying too hard to convince this prosecutor of the legitimacy of a defense – usually this type of prosecutor sees the legitimacy or sees the bluff. In cases where there are legitimate issues this prosecutor will usually bend because they understand the issues at hand. Additionally, there may be a relationship between this prosecutor and your attorney because of the prosecutor's longevity. On the other hand, if your case lacks any real defenses, it may be difficult for your attorney to bluster or bully his way to a better deal.

Career prosecutor's can be found in district and municipal courts although if they are to be found in district court it is likely that it is in a small county because in larger counties career prosecutors graduate to Superior court (felonies) before too long.

The Businessman

The businessman is only found in the Municipal court setting. Typically this is the prosecutor who has the contract with the city and is a prosecuting attorney in this environment as a means to earn more money than as a prosecutor in a similar county level. It is fair to say that the majority of these prosecutors are businessmen first and prosecuting attorney's second. Additionally they almost always have many years experience so it is not easy to pull a fast one. Alternatively, because they are businessman they also realize that they must be efficient with their case load because they do not get paid any more if they go to trial. Hence, these prosecutors are quite realistic in dealing with cases and realize that there must be some give and take. However, it can never be forgotten that due to the fact that they have a contract with the City they must continue to please those who hire him. From my experience the majority of these prosecutors are generally reasonable to deal with.

The Power Monger

This is the prosecutor to be wary of. This prosecutor enjoys having the power of deciding the outcomes of people's cases and affecting people's lives. With this type of prosecutor it is very important that your attorney is aware of what makes this prosecutor tick. Playing to his ego is sometimes the way to get a deal done. This type of attorney is found at both district court and municipal court.

The Judge

The Judge's role in a case is a rather intriguing one. As a DUI attorney I am always aware of the Judge and his reputation and how his role may affect my client and my client's case. That being said, the Judge's role can at times be rather limited during a DUI case. However, when called on the Judge's role may be critical to the outcome of your case. Furthermore, knowing how a Judge rules on certain legal issues may (or may not) give you an advantage in plea negotiating.

The first time most come into contact with the Judge is at the arraignment. At this stage the Judge will determine if you are to be taken into custody or released on your own "personal recognizance." (P.R.) It is important for your attorney to know the Judge and what his practice is regarding taking DUI defendants into custody. Additionally, if you are taken into custody it will be the Judge who determines what the bail amount will be. Again, it is important to know the Judge's practice regarding bail and the amount generally ordered. Finally, if the Judge permits release (which is typical) he will then determine what conditions will be imposed. The conditions will usually be no driving unless licensed and insured, no consuming alcohol, and no refusing a breath test if lawfully requested of you. Once again, knowledge is everything and the more your attorney knows about the Judge the better prepared you will be.

Judges will also decide whether or not to grant requested

continuances. This may be of some significance and your attorney should be familiar with the policies of the sitting Judge. Of more importance is how the Judge rules on issues relating to the suppression of the breath test, probable cause to stop and arrest, and the usual motion issues that are raised at suppression hearings.

The Judge's role is perhaps most significant during a motion hearing. At such a hearing your attorney argues certain legal issues in your case and requests the Judge to suppress evidence. Knowing a Judge's tendencies and rulings may profoundly affect the outcome of such a motion and ultimately your case.

Finally, Judge's have significance at sentencing. Usually there is an agreement regarding sentencing and if both the prosecutor and you (through your attorney) agree on a sentence it is likely that the Judge will follow the recommendations. Importantly, the Judge will inform you that despite the agreement the Judge does not have to follow the agreement and may sentence you up to the maximum penalties. Before agreeing to any sentence be certain that your attorney has confidence that the Judge will follow the agreement and what you can do, if anything, to ensure the Judge accepts the agreement.

Plea Negotiating

Plea negotiating is where your attorney discusses your case with the prosecutor and receives an offer. Your attorney will discuss the offer with you then convey to the prosecutor that you reject the offer, or discuss the offer with you and then convey to the prosecutor that you will accept the offer. Plea negotiating is simply your attorney discussing (or arguing) the merits of your case with the prosecutor and then determining if an agreement can be put together.

Most defense attorneys approach plea negotiating in slightly different ways and there is probably no absolutely correct approach. There is one improper way to conduct plea negotiating and this is to accept the first offer provided by the prosecutor. The first offer is usually not the best offer and is almost never worth accepting. It is your attorney's job to investigate your case completely and push the prosecutor until breaking point to determine what the best offer will ultimately be. However, that being said, it is also possible that there will never be an offer worth accepting. If your attorney is an experienced and well trained DUI attorney he will know what will be a reasonable offer well before talking to the prosecuting attorney.

Each defense attorney has their own style of negotiating with a prosecuting attorney. Some attorneys approach prosecutor's with aggression from the beginning. They immediately reject the first offer and set your case for motions to determine the legitimacy of any and all outstanding issues that exist in your case. Setting motions to determine the legitimacy of the stop, field sobriety tests, your statements, the arrest, and the breath or blood test immediately forces the prosecutor into a defensive posture and forces them to deal with your case from the outset. This can be a great way to pressure the prosecutor into a deal as such a motion requires more work and the presence of the arresting officer (meaning the State Patrol or City Police may have the pay the officer overtime). If there are legitimate issues, this is a good approach. However, if there are no seriously legitimate issues this approach may backfire and upset the prosecutor to the point where no deal will be offered. Further, if there are no legitimate issues, your attorney may lose some credibility with the prosecuting attorney.

Another approach is for the defense attorney, if no good deal is offered, to set the case for trial hoping that the prosecutor will deal because of a heavy trial schedule. This sometimes works but should only be used as a last case resort. There is a risk in doing this because the prosecutor may add additional charges against you, so proceed with caution when setting cases for trial.

The approach I use in most cases is as follows. First, before I proceed I make sure I know who the prosecutor is. If I know the prosecutor, which is often the case, I will know what approach to use. In most cases I will not contact the prosecuting attorney until all of my investigation and preparation has occurred. At that point I send a detailed letter to the prosecutor arguing the legal defenses and issues in the case and also outlining who my client is. Detailing the legal issues is done in a straight forward manner that emphasizes the weaknesses in the prosecutor's case. This is very important as prosecutors do not have the time (or inclination) to spend the time necessary to look very closely into each case. Therefore if the issues can be clearly presented it may alone be persuasive enough to get an acceptable offer from the prosecutor.

In addition to the legal issues I believe it is important to humanize my clients. The reason is that to a prosecutor you are just another DUI charge, faceless, and not human. Truth be told, this is not a very strong way to approach a case, but it still amazes how many prosecutors will give you a better a deal if they learn that you are a decent person, have children, an important job, no alcohol dependency (or if you do, have started treatment immediately), and have significant involvement in the community, and so on. I have always maintained that DUI cases are 99% legal and 1% human. But that 1% is vitally important and cannot be overlooked when negotiating a case.

If I am still unable to get an acceptable offer after corresponding with the prosecutor I will immediately set my client's case for motions. This will then put pressure on the prosecutor to deal with your case. Once motions are set I frequently get a better offer prior to the motion date. However, if I am unable to get a better offer we proceed to motions and argue to the Judge to suppress (exclude) certain evidence in the case based on legitimate legal theories.

After the motion hearing, if certain evidence is suppressed I again approach the prosecutor and argue for a better offer. At that point if I am unable to get a better offer I meet with my client to discuss their options, which could be to accept the best offer from the prosecutor or set the case for trial.

Finally, I ensure that my clients are well advised of the possible outcomes in their case from the first moment I meet with them. Therefore the offers from the prosecutor should not be surprising and my client is prepared from the outset. Although acceptable deals are typical, one has to be mindful of being realistic too.

CHAPTER 10

Alcohol, Drugs and the Human Body

Alcohol's Properties

When most people think of alcohol the first thing that comes into their minds is a cold beer, a full bodied cabernet, or a martini. Although this perception is not incorrect, more properly alcohol is part of a family of organic chemicals that include ethanol, methanol, and isopropanol, to name only a few. The most commonly ingested of these three examples is ethanol.

Alcohol (ethanol) is a central nervous system depressant and it is the central nervous system which is the bodily system that is most harshly affected by the ingestion of alcohol. The degree that the central nervous system function is affected depends of the concentration of alcohol in the blood stream.

When alcohol is consumed it passes from the stomach into the small intestine and is then rapidly absorbed into the blood stream. It is distributed through the body quickly and because of that it does not require a large concentration to have an affect.

Absorption

The human body absorbs alcohol from all parts of the gastrointestinal tract largely by distribution into the blood stream. The small intestine, however, is by far the most efficient region of the gastrointestinal tract for alcohol absorption because of its very large surface area. Complete absorption of alcohol that results in peak alcohol concentration can take between 0.75 to 6 hours, depending on the amount of food in your stomach, although the average is between 1 and 2.5 hours.

Distribution

Alcohol is attracted to water and as a result can be found in body tissues and fluids because they contain water. Once the alcohol is absorbed it is then carried quickly though the body in the blood. When the alcohol is completely absorbed in the body there is approximately the same concentration of alcohol in the blood stream.

Elimination

Most of the alcohol in the body is eliminated by the liver, through metabolism. This type of elimination accounts for approximately 95 %. The remainder is eliminated by the body in the breath, urine, sweat, feces, and saliva.

Generally, a normal individual eliminates an average of one normal drink of alcohol per hour. This rate can vary and typically the rate of elimination tends to be higher when the blood alcohol concentration in the body is very high or very low. Additionally, conditioned alcoholics may (depending on liver health) eliminate alcohol in their body at a significantly higher rate than the average individual. Lastly, the body's ability to eliminate alcohol quickly tends to lessen with age.

Body Weight and Body Type

Generally, the less you weigh the more you will be affected by alcohol. For people who weigh the same, a person with more muscle will be affected less than a person with more fat. This is because fatty tissue does not contain much water and therefore does not absorb very much alcohol.

Alcohol Content

While the number of drinks you consume does have a role in determining how much alcohol content is in your system, it is also dependent on how much alcohol content is in the drinks you consume. Below is a list of common alcoholic beverages and their alcohol content:

Alcohol Content (in Percent) of Selected Beverages

Beverage	Alcohol Content %
Beers (lager)	3.2 - 4.0
Malt Liquor	3.2 - 7.0
Ales	4.5
Porter	6.0
Stout	6.0 - 8.0
Table wines	7.1 - 14.0
Sparkling wines	8.0 - 14.0
Sake	14.0 - 16.0

Brandies	40.0 - 43.0
Whiskies	40.0 - 75.0
Vodkas	40.0 - 50.0
Gin	40.0 - 48.5
Rum	40.0 - 95.0
Tequila	45.0 - 50.5

The table "Alcohol Content (in Percent) of Selected Beverages" is from Chapter 1, "Chemistry of Alcoholic Beverages", Bill H. McAnalley.

Food

If you mix food with alcohol the result will be a lower and delayed blood alcohol concentration. There are two major factors involved.

First, the ingestion of food slows down the absorption of alcohol because alcohol is absorbed most quickly when it passes into the body through the stomach. When a person eats food the pyloric valve at the bottom of the stomach will close in order to hold food in the stomach for digestion. This keeps the alcohol from reaching the stomach and as a result alcohol will travel through the small intestine and be absorbed into the body this way. This ultimately results in a lower alcohol concentration (hence a lower BAC). Second, because there are lower levels of alcohol in your system due to food ingestion the body eliminates the alcohol absorbed at a faster rate.

The types of food eaten does not seem to have any significant affect, but the larger the meal and closer in time between eating and drinking, generally results in a lower alcohol concentration.

Medication

Mixing medication and alcohol is never wise and in many instances it could and does increase the effects of alcohol. It is highly recommended that you never mix alcohol and drugs and it is equally wise to consult with a physician if are on medication and considering consuming alcohol. Moreover, it is also illegal to drive under the combined affect of both alcohol and drugs (legal or illegal).

Fatigue

Fatigue can cause many of the same symptoms as alcohol intoxication. If you are suffering from fatigue it is wise not to consume excessive alcohol as you many only amplify these symptoms.

Tolerance

Tolerance is the reduction of the efficiency of alcohol over a period of extended or heavy use of alcohol. There are two types of tolerance at work with alcohol, metabolic tolerance and functional tolerance.

Metabolic tolerance is when alcohol is metabolized at a faster rate in chronic users. With this type of tolerance individuals have lower peak blood alcohol concentrations than average drinkers when the same amount of alcohol is consumed.

Functional tolerance is when there is an actual change in the organ or system's sensitivity to alcohol. There have been studies that have shown that chronic alcoholics can have twice the tolerance for alcohol as an average person.

Gender Differences

Generally (but certainly not always) women tend to have a higher percentage of body fat and therefore a lower percentage of body water. Assuming this is correct, if a man and a woman of the same weight consume the same amount of alcohol the woman will tend to have a higher alcohol concentration. Obviously this would not be the case if the woman was very fit and the man was obese, but on average, this is the case. Additionally, total body water tends to diminish with age, so an older person will also be more affected by the same amount of alcohol due to less body water.

Another difference between men and women is in the elimination of alcohol. There are studies that show that women discharge alcohol from their bodies at a rate 10% greater than that of men.

Blood Alcohol Concentration (B.A.C.) Chart
(Percent of Alcohol in Bloodstream)

Body weight	NUMBER OF DRINKS CONSUMED									
	1	2	3	4	5	6	7	8	9	10
100 lb.	.038	.075	.113	.150	.188	.225	.263	.300	.338	.375
120 lb.	.031	.063	.094	.125	.156	.188	.219	.250	.281	.313
140 lb.	.027	.054	.080	.107	.134	.161	.188	.214	.241	.268
160 lb.	.023	.047	.070	.094	.117	.141	.164	.188	.211	.234
180 lb.	.021	.042	.063	.083	.104	.125	.146	.167	.188	.208
200 lb.	.019	.038	.056	.075	.094	.113	.131	.150	.169	.188
220 lb.	.017	.034	.051	.068	.085	.102	.119	.136	.153	.170
240 lb.	.016	.031	.047	.063	.078	.094	.109	.125	.141	.156

[Data from NHTSA chart, with modifications]

Drugs and the DUI

Alcohol and its effect on the human body have been well studied and researched in the DUI context. Moreover, the emphasis of NHTSA and law enforcement over the past century has been on curbing the number of alcohol related DUIs by means of DUI emphasis patrols, educating the public and training their officers. However, the impact that drugs have on individuals and its relation to driving under the influence has been poorly studied and law enforcement has been slow to respond.

In the DUI field drug DUIs are steadily becoming more common place. Although the detection by law enforcement of drugs in the driver's system is still relatively poor, law enforcement is slowly attempting to educate their offices to detect certain drugs. The most common drugs found in DUI drivers and their effect on the driver are listed below.

Morphine

Morphine is a highly potent opiate analgesic drug and is the principal active agent in opium. Morphine is considered to be the prototypical opioid. Like other opioids (e.g. oxycodone, hydromorphone, and diacetylmorphine (heroin)), morphine acts directly on the central nervous system (CNS) to relieve pain.

The effects created by morphine include euphoria and the feeling of well-being, relaxation, drowsiness, sedation, lethargy, disconnectedness, self-absorption, mental clouding, and delirium. Couper, Fiona J., and Logan, Barry K. *Drugs and Human Performance Fact Sheets*. NHTSA. Page 76-77 (March 2004) When mixed with alcohol sedation, drowsiness, and decreased motor skills may occur. *Id.* According to NHTSA, in several driving under the influence case reports where the subjects tested positive for morphine, observations included slow driving, weaving, poor vehicle control, poor coordination, slow response to stimuli, delayed reactions, difficultly in following instructions, and falling asleep at the wheel. *Id.*

In the DUI context and field sobriety testing, horizontal gaze nystagmus, vertical gaze nystagmus, and lack of convergence are not present. Further, pupil size is constricted and there is little or no reaction to light. The subject's pulse rate, blood pressure, and body temperature are generally lower. *Id.*

Heroin

Diacetylmorphine (better known as heroin) is another derivative of the opium poppy, and was synthesized from morphine in 1874 by C. R. Alder Wright, an English chemist working at St. Mary's Hospital Medical School in London, England. Heroin was subsequently brought to market by the pharmaceutical giant Bayer, in 1898. From 1898 through to 1910, heroin was marketed as a non-addictive morphine substitute and cough suppressant. Bayer marketed heroin as a cure for morphine addiction before it was discovered that it is rapidly metabolized into morphine, and as such, heroin was essentially a quicker acting form of morphine. Bayer was understandably embarrassed by this finding and it soon became an historical blunder for the company. Bayer lost some of its trademark rights to "heroin," as it did with aspirin (and other drugs), under the 1919 Treaty of Versailles following the German defeat in World War I. *Treaty of Versailles*, Part X, Section IV, Article 298. Annex, Paragraph 5. (June 28, 1919)

Heroin is nearly twice as potent as morphine and as with

other opioids heroin is used as both a pain-killer and a recreational drug.

The effects created by heroin are very much the same as those created by the use of morphine and include euphoria and the feeling of well-being, relaxation, drowsiness, sedation, lethargy, disconnectedness, self-absorption, mental clouding, and delirium. Couper, Fiona J., and Logan, Barry K. *Drugs and Human Performance Fact Sheets*. NHTSA. Page 76-77 (March 2004)

In the DUI context and field sobriety testing, horizontal gaze nystagmus, vertical gaze nystagmus, and lack of convergence are not present. Further, pupil size is constricted and there is little or no reaction to light. The subject's pulse rate, blood pressure, and body temperature are generally lower. *Id.*

Methadone

Methadone is a synthetic opioid used medically as an analgesic, antitussive and as a maintenance anti-addictive for use in patients on opioids. The drug was developed in 1937 in Nazi Germany and although chemically unlike morphine or heroin, methadone also acts on the opioid receptors and thus produces similar effects. The drug was given the trade name "dolophine" from the Latin *dolor* meaning pain

The effects created by the use of methadone include drowsiness, sedation, dizziness, lightheadedness, mood swings (euphoria to dysphoria), depressed reflexes, altered sensory perception, stupor, and coma. Couper, Fiona J., and Logan, Barry K. *Drugs and Human Performance Fact Sheets*. NHTSA. Page 57-58 (March 2004)

The drug manufacturer cautions that methadone may impair the mental and/or physical abilities required for the performance of potentially hazardous tasks, and that the sedative effects of the drug may be enhanced by concurrent use of other CNS depressants, including alcohol.

In the DUI context and field sobriety testing, horizontal gaze nystagmus, vertical gaze nystagmus, and lack of convergence are not present. Pupil size is constricted and there is little to no reaction to light. Pulse rate, blood pressure, and body temperature are lower.

Oxycodone

Oxycodone is an opioid synthesized from opium-derived thebaine. It was developed in 1916 in Germany by Freund and Speyer of the University of Frankfurt, only a few years after pharmaceutical company Bayer had stopped the mass production of heroin due to addiction and abuse. It was hoped that a thebaine-derived drug would retain the analgesic effects of morphine and heroin with less addiction. The first clinical use of the drug was documented in 1917. Sunshine, A., Olson, N.Z., Colon, A., Rivera, J., Kaiko, R.F., Fitzmartin, R.D., Reder, R.F., Goldenheim, P.D. (1996). *Analgesic efficacy of controlled-release oxycodone in postoperative pain. J Clin Pharmacol* 36 (7): 595–603 (1996)

The drug was first introduced to the US market in 1939 and is the active ingredient in a number of pain medications commonly prescribed for the relief of moderate to severe pain, either with inert binders (e.g. OxyContin) or supplemental analgesics such as paracetamol (acetaminophen), (e.g. Percocet, Endocet, Tylox, Roxicet) or aspirin (e.g. Percodan, Endodan, Roxiprin). More recently, ibuprofen has been added to oxycodone under the name Combunox.

Hydrocodone

Hydrocodone is a semi-synthetic opioid derived from two of the naturally occurring opiates *codeine* and *thebaine*. It is marketed, in its varying forms, under a number of trademarks, including Vicodin. Hydrocodone was first synthesized in Germany in 1920 and was approved by the FDA on March 23, 1943 for sale in the United States under the brand name Hycodan. http://www.fda.gov/

As a narcotic, hydrocodone relieves pain by binding to opioid receptors in the brain and spinal cord. Common side effects that drivers should be concerned about include dizziness, lightheadedness, nausea, and drowsiness.

Cocaine

Cocaine (benzoylmethyl ecgonine) is a crystalline tropane alkaloid that is obtained from the leaves of the coca plant. Aggrawal, Anil. *Narcotic Drugs*. National Book Trust, India. (1995) The name, cocaine, comes from "coca" in addition to the alkaloid suffix "ine," forming "cocaine" and is both a stimulant of the central nervous system and an appetite suppressant.

Other uses for cocaine include its use as a treatment for morphine addiction in the late 1800s. Cocaine was introduced into clinical use as a local anesthetic in Germany at about the same time. By the turn of the twentieth century, the addictive properties of cocaine had become obvious and the problem of cocaine abuse began to capture public attention in the United States.

Currently, cocaine is the second most popular illegal recreational drug in the U.S. (behind marijuana) and the U.S. is the world's largest consumer of cocaine. Central Intelligence Agency, *The World Factbook – Illicit Drugs.* (March 19, 2009)

The effects caused by the use of cocaine include euphoria, excitation, feelings of well-being, general arousal, increased sexual excitement, dizziness, self-absorbed, increased focus and alertness, mental clarity, increased talkativeness, motor restlessness, offsets fatigue, improved performance in some simple tasks, and loss of appetite. Higher doses may exhibit a pattern of psychosis with confused and disoriented behavior, delusions, hallucinations, irritability, fear, paranoia, antisocial behavior, and aggressiveness. Couper, Fiona J., and Logan, Barry K. *Drugs and Human Performance Fact Sheets.* NHTSA. Page 19 (March 2004)

According to NHTSA the observed signs of impairment in driving performance have included subjects speeding, losing control of their vehicle, causing collisions, turning in front of other vehicles, high-risk behavior, inattentive driving, and poor impulse control. As the effects of cocaine wear off subjects may suffer from fatigue, depression, sleepiness, and inattention.

In the DUI context as it relates to field sobriety testing, horizontal gaze nystagmus, vertical gaze nystagmus, and lack of convergence are not present. Pupil size is dilated and there is a slow reaction to light. Pulse rate, blood pressure elevated, and body temperature are elevated.

Independent studies seem to contradict some of the findings by NHTSA. These studies have found that cocaine increases alertness, consciousness, energy levels, pulse rate, body temperature, and glucose availability (energy for the body), and has been found to counteract effects of fatigue and alcohol consumption. Rush, C.R., Baker, R.W., and Wright, K. *Acute Physiological and Behavioral Effects of Oral Cocaine in*

Humans: A dose response analysis. Drug Alcohol Depend. 55. Pages 1-12 (1999); Stillman, R. Jones, R.T., Moore, J, Walker, J., and Welm, S. *Improved Performance Four Hours After Cocaine.* Psychopharmacology. 110. Pages 415-420 (1993); Farre, M., et al. *Alcohol and Cocaine Interactions in Humans.* J Pharmacol Exp Ther. 266. Pages 1364-1373 (1993); Higgins, S.T., et al. *Acute Behavioral and Cardiac Effects of Cocaine and Alcohol Combinations in Humans.* Psychopharmacology. 111. Pages 285-294 (1993)

Another concern with cocaine is when it is consumed in conjunction with alcohol. When the two are mixed an active metabolite of "cocaethylene" is produced. This specific metabolite has a longer half-life than cocaine when the drug is taken by itself. Cani, J. et al. *Cocaine metabolism in humans after use of alcohol: Clinical and Research Implications.* Recent Developments in Alcohol. No. 14, Pages 437-455 (1998)

Moskowitz and Burns conducted a study looking at the effects of cocaine consumption and driving performance and concluded that there was no impairment of driving-related laboratory tasks by cocaine (cocaine consumption was intranasally, 96 mg). Moskowitz, H. and Burns, M. *The Effects of a Single, Acute Dose of Cocaine Upon Driving-Related Skills Performance.* T89, 11th International Conference on Alcohol, Drugs and Traffic Safety. (1989)

Marijuana

Cannabis, also known as marijuana, is a psychoactive drug extracted from the plant "Cannabis sativa." The herbal form of the drug consists of dried mature flowers and subtending leaves of pistillate (female) plants and the major biologically active chemical compound in cannabis is Δ^9-tetrahydrocannabinol (delta-9-tetrahydrocannabinol), commonly referred to as THC.

People have been consuming cannabis for thousands of years although the last one hundred years has seen an increase in its use for recreational, religious or spiritual, and medicinal purposes. Rudgley, Richard. *Lost Civilisations of the Stone Age.* (1998). The possession, use, or sale of psychoactive cannabis products became illegal in most parts of the world in the early 20th century.

The use of cannabis, at least as fiber, has been shown to go back at least 10,000 years in Taiwan. Stafford, Peter. *Psychedelics Encyclopedia.* Ronin Publishing (1993) Today recreational use in the western world drives a sizable demand for the drug. Cannabis is the largest cash crop in the United States generating an estimated $36 billion market. *"Marijuana Called Top U.S. Cash Crop".* ABCNews Internet Ventures. (2008)

The effects caused by the use of marijuana include relaxation, euphoria, relaxed inhibitions, sense of well-being, disorientation, altered time and space perception, lack of concentration, impaired learning and memory, alterations in thought formation and expression, drowsiness, sedation, mood changes such as panic reactions and paranoia, and a more vivid sense of taste, sight, smell, and hearing. Couper, Fiona J., and Logan, Barry K. *Drugs and Human Performance Fact Sheets.* NHTSA. Page 7 (March 2004) Additionally, when taken concurrently with alcohol, marijuana is more likely to be a traffic safety risk factor than when consumed alone. *Id.*

In the DUI context relating to field sobriety testing, horizontal gaze nystagmus and vertical gaze nystagmus are not present although lack of convergence is present. Pupil size is normal to dilated and the reaction to light is normal to slow. Pulse rate and blood pressure are elevated and body temperature normal to elevated.

Naturally, there are critics who suggest that the combination of marijuana consumption and driving is not nearly as dangerous as alcohol and drugs. Certain driving studies actually suggest that marijuana users are more cautious, slow down, drive more safely and take fewer risks compared to alcohol users. Kruger, H.P. and Berghaus, G. *Behavioral Effects of Alcohol and Cannabis: Can Equipontoncies by Established?* Center for Traffic Sciences, University of Wurzburg, Rontgenring. 11, D-97070. Wurzburg, Germany; Robbe, H. *Marijuana's Effects on Actual Driving Performance.* In: Kloeden, C. and McLean, A (Eds). *Alcohol, Drugs and Traffic Safety T-95.* Adelaide, Australia: HHMRC Road Research Unit, University of Adelaide. Pages 11-20 (1995) Interestingly a NHTSA study concluded the following: "THC's adverse effects on driving performance appear relatively small." Hindrik, W, Robbe, J., O'Hanlon, J. *Marijuana and Actual Driving Performance.* Washington, D.C. U.S. Department of Transportation, National Highway Traffic Safety Administration. Report No. DOT HS 88 078 (1973)

Methanmpehtamine

Methamphetamine, or simply "Meth," is a psychostimulant and sympathomimetic drug. It is a member of the family of phenylethylamines and is used for weight loss and to maintain alertness, focus, motivation, and mental clarity for extended periods of time, and also for recreational purposes.

The drug was first synthesized from ephedrine in Japan in 1894 by chemist Nagai, Nagayoshi. Nagai, N. *"Kanyaku maou seibun kenkyuu seiseki (zoku)".* Yakugaku Zashi *13: 901.* (1893) In 1919, crystallized methamphetamine was synthesized by Akira Ogata via reduction of ephedrine using red phosphorus and iodine. One of the earliest uses of methamphetamine was during World War II when the German military widely distributed the drug in chocolates dosed with methamphetamine. These chocolates were known as "fliegerschokolade" ("flyer's chocolate") when given to pilots, or "panzerschokolade" ("tanker's chocolate") when given to tank crews. It has been long rumored that from 1942 until his death in 1945, Adolf Hitler may have been injected with methamphetamine by his personal physician Theodor Morell as a treatment for depression and fatigue. Doyle, D. *Hitler's Medical Care.* Journal of the Royal College of Physicians of Edinburgh. 35: 75–82. (2005)

The effects of methamphetamine include euphoria, excitation, exhilaration, rapid flight of ideas, increased libido, rapid speech, motor restlessness, hallucinations, delusions, psychosis, insomnia, reduced fatigue or drowsiness, increased alertness, heightened sense of well being, stereotypes behavior, feelings of increased physical strength, and poor impulse control. Couper, Fiona J., and Logan, Barry K. *Drugs and Human Performance Fact Sheets.* NHTSA. Page 63 (March 2004) However, during the late phase of consumption of this drug the effects change and include fatigue, sleepiness with sudden starts, itching/picking/scratching, normal heart rate, and normal to small pupils which are reactive to light.

In the DUI context as it relates to field sobriety testing, horizontal gaze nystagmus, vertical gaze nystagmus, and lack of convergence are not present. Pupil size is dilated and there is a slow reaction to light. Pulse rate and blood pressure is elevated and body temperature normal to lower.

Generally it is conceded that methamphetamine is not usually a major cause of impairment in DUI situations. This is so because it is a stimulant and the time where the drug is active does not seem to cause great concern with researchers. However, the "hangover" effects are of more concern. Logan, B.K. *Methamphetamine and Driving Impairment.* J. Forensic Sci. 41:457-464 (1996) This study reported that methamphetamine users exhibited improved reaction time, relief from fatigue, and euphoria. *Id.* Further, an earlier study also concluded that therapeutic doses of amphetamine are no threat to traffic safety and may actually improve performance. Hurst, P.M. *Amphetamines and driving.* Alcohol, Drugs and Driving. 3:13-17 (1987) To confuse matters even more, an earlier study yet found there to be a high rate of traffic accidents among amphetamine abusers. Smart, R. G., Schmidt, W. and Bateman, K. *Psychoactive drugs and traffic accidents.* J. Safety Res. 1, 67-73 (1969)

In summary the effects of this drug seem to depend on the dose. At lower doses amphetamines have few effects on cognitive functioning but at higher doses risk-taking increases. Sherwood, N. *A critical review of the effects of drugs other than alcohol on driving.* Automobile Association (UK) Report. (Unpublished) (1998)

MDMA (Ecstasy)

MDMA (3,4-methylenedioxy-N-methamphetamine), or commonly known as "ecstasy" (or abbreviated E, X, or XTC), is a semisynthetic member of the amphetamine class of psychoactive drugs, a subclass of the phenethylamines.

Ecstacy's euphoric tendency produces a sense of intimacy with others and diminished feelings of fear and anxiety. Ecstacy is criminalized in all countries in the world under a UN agreement, but despite this it is one of the most widely used illicit drugs in the world. It is commonly associated with the rave culture and its related genres of music.

The effects after consuming Ecstacy include mild intoxication, relaxation, euphoria, an excited calm or peace, feelings
of well-being, increase in physical and emotional energy,
increased sociability and closeness, heightened sensitivity,
increased responsiveness to touch, changes in perception,
and empathy. At higher doses, agitation, panic attacks, and il-
lusory or hallucinatory experiences may occur. Couper, Fiona
J., and Logan, Barry K. *Drugs and Human Performance Fact
Sheets*. NHTSA. Page 68 (March 2004)

In the DUI context as it relates to field sobriety testing,
horizontal gaze nystagmus, vertical gaze nystagmus, and lack
of convergence are not present. Pupil size is dilated and there
is a slow reaction to light. Pulse rate is elevated while blood
pressure and body temperature are normal to elevated.

To date, no studies have directly examined Ecstacy's effects on driving performance, although there are a few which
have looked at cognitive and perceptual effects, which may
have relevance to driving. One such study described the case
of a young female who developed panic disorder after multiple ingestion of Ecstacy. Windhaber, J., Maierhofer, D., and
Dantendorfer. *Panic order induced by large doses of 3,4-meth-
ylenedioxymethamphetamine resolved by paroxetine*. J. Clin.
Psychopharmacol. 18(1), 95-6. (1998) And it is this type of
unpredictable side-effect which make ecstasy a potential danger amongst drivers.

Lysergic Acid Diethylamide (LSD)

Lysergic acid diethylamide, otherwise known as LSD,
LSD-25, or simply acid, is a semisynthetic psychedelic drug
of the ergoline family. Its unusual psychological effects which
include visuals of colored patterns behind the eyes in the

mind, a sense of time distorting, and crawling geometric patterns have made it one of the most widely known psychedelic drugs. It has been used mainly as a recreational drug, and as a tool to supplement various practices for transcendence, meditation, psychonautics, art projects, and illicit (formerly legal) psychedelic therapy.

LSD is synthesized from lysergic acid derived from ergot, a grain fungus that typically grows on rye, and was first synthesized in November 16, 1938 by Swiss chemist Albert Hofmann at the Sandoz Laboratories in Switzerland. Its psychedelic properties were unknown until five years later, when Hofmann, acting on what he has called a "peculiar presentiment," returned to work on the chemical. Nichols, David. *Hypothesis on Albert Hofmann's Famous 1943 "Bicycle Day".* Hofmann Foundation. (2003)

The effects after consuming LSD are unpredictable and will depend on the dose ingested, the user's personality and mood, expectations and the surroundings. Couper, Fiona J., and Logan, Barry K. *Drugs and Human Performance Fact Sheets.* NHTSA. Page 52 (March 2004)

However, the effects typically include hallucinations, increased color perception, altered mental state, thought disorders, temporary psychosis, delusions, body image changes, and impaired depth, time and space perceptions. Users may feel several emotions at once or swing rapidly from one emotion to another. "Bad trips" may consist of severe, terrifying thoughts and feelings, fear of losing control, and despair.

In the DUI context as it relates to field sobriety testing, horizontal gaze nystagmus, vertical gaze nystagmus, and lack of convergence are not present. Pupil size is dilated and the reaction to light is normal. Pulse rate, blood pressure, and body temperature are elevated.

Gamma-Hydroxybutyrate (GHB)

Hydroxybutyric acid, 4-hydroxybutanoic acid, GHB, but commonly known as "the date rape drug," is a naturally-occurring substance found in the central nervous system, wine, beef, small citrus fruits, and almost all animals in small amounts. Weil, Andrew; Winifred Rosen. "Depressants". From Chocolate to Morphine. (2nd edition ed.). Boston/New York: Houghton Mifflin Company. Page. 77 (1993) GHB was first synthesized in 1960 as an experimental GABA analog, and was classified as a food and dietary supplement and sold in health food stores in early 1990. GHB is illegal in many countries and is currently regulated in the US and is used to treat cataplexy and excessive daytime sleepiness in patients with narcolepsy.

GHB is a CNS depressant used as an intoxicant. At recreational doses, GHB can cause a state of euphoria, increased enjoyment of movement and music, increased libido, increased sociability and intoxication. At higher doses GHB may induce nausea, dizziness, drowsiness, agitation, visual disturbances, depressed breathing, amnesia, unconsciousness, and death.

The effects observed after having consumed GHB are similar to those effects observed with alcohol consumption. Couper, Fiona J., and Logan, Barry K. *Drugs and Human Performance Fact Sheets*. NHTSA. Page 42 (March 2004) These include relaxation, reduced inhibitions, euphoria, confusion, dizziness, drowsiness, sedation, inebriation, agitation, combativeness, and hallucinations.

In the DUI context as it relates to field sobriety testing, horizontal gaze nystagmus, vertical gaze nystagmus (in high doses), and lack of convergence are present. Pupil size is generally dilated and reaction to light is slow. Pulse rate and blood pressure are normal and body temperature is generally down.

Sedatives/Sleeping Pills

Sedatives are substances that induce sedation by reducing "irritability or excitement." At higher doses the user may experience slurred speech, staggering gait, poor judgment, and slow, uncertain reflexes.

All Sedatives can cause physiological and psychological dependence when taken regularly over a period of time, even at therapeutic doses. Barondes, Samuel H. *Better Than Prozac.* New York: Oxford University Press. Pages 47–59 (2003).; Mant, A, Whicker, SD, McManus, P, Birkett, DJ, Edmonds D, Dumbrell D. *"Benzodiazepine utilisation in Australia: report from a new pharmacoepidemiological database."* Aust J Public Health. 17 (4): 345–9 (December 1993)

Sedatives are divided into barbiturates, benzodiazepines (clonazepam (Klonopin)), diazepam (Valium), and alprazolam (Xanax) are a few examples)), herbal sedatives (ie. kava, cannabis), solvent sedatives (ie.diethyl ether (Ether), ethyl alcohol (alcoholic beverage)), methyl trichloride (Chloroform), non-benzodiazepine sedatives (eszopiclone (Lunesta), zaleplon (Sonata), zolpidem (Ambien)), and uncategorized sedatives (ie. gamma-hydroxybutyrate (GHB), diphenhydramine (Benadryl), methaqualone (Quaalude)).

Diazepam (Valium)

Diazepam, a benzodiazepine, was approved for use in 1960 and in 1963 its improved version, valium, was released and became very popular helping its manufacturer, Roche, become a pharmaceutical industry giant. Valium is two and a half times more potent than its predecessor, chlordiazepoxide, which it quickly surpassed in terms of sales. After this initial success, other pharmaceutical companies began to introduce other benzodiazepine derivatives.

Diazepam was the top-selling pharmaceutical in the United States from 1969 to 1982, with peak sales in 1978 of 2.3 billion tablets. Sample, Ian. *Leo Steinbach's Obituary.* The Guardian (Guardian Unlimited) (October 3, 2005)

The effects observed after consumption of valium at low doses include sleepiness, drowsiness, confusion, and some loss of intergraded memory. Couper, Fiona J., and Logan, Barry K. *Drugs and Human Performance Fact Sheets.* NHTSA. Page 31 (March 2004) Diazepam can produce a state of intoxication similar to that of alcohol, including slurred speech, disorientation, and drunken behavior. *Id.*

In the DUI context as it relates to field sobriety testing, horizontal gaze nystagmus, vertical gaze nystagmus (in high doses), and lack of convergence are present. Pupil size is normal and reaction to light is slow. Pulse rate and blood pressure are down and body temperature is normal. *Id.*

Alprazolam (Xanax)

Alprazolam, also known under the trade name Xanax, is a short-acting drug of the benzodiazepine class used to treat anxiety disorders, panic attacks, and anxiety associated with moderate depression.

Alprazolam was first synthesized by Upjohn (now a part of Pfizer) in 1969 and was first produced for use in 1976. Dangers in the context of DUI would be side effects that include drowsiness (common), dizziness (common), lightheadedness (common), fatigue, unsteadiness and impaired coordination, vertigo, slurred speech, and short-term memory loss and impairment of memory functions. Rawson, N.S., Rawson, M.J. *Acute adverse event signaling scheme using the Saskatchewan Administrative health care utilization datafiles: results for two benzodiazepines.* Can J Clin Pharmacol 6 (3): 159–66 (1999)

Eszopiclone (Lunesta)

Eszopiclone, best known as Lunesta, is a nonbenzodiazepine hypnotic agent (sedative) used as a treatment for insomnia. Lunesta, along with other related drugs, including Ambien and Sonata are the most commonly prescribed sedative hypnotics in the United State. There were 43 million prescriptions issued for insomnia medications during 2005 in the USA which generated a total of $2.7 billion for pharmaceutical companies. McKenzie, W.S. and Rosenberg M. *What every dentist should know about the z-sedatives.* J Mass Dent Soc 56 (53): 44–5 (2007)

It has been reported that people who have taken this prescription have engaged in activity such as driving, eating, or making phone calls and later having no memory of the activity. Lunesta can also cause side effects that impair thinking or reaction times.

Zaleplon (Sonata)

Zaleplon (marketed under the brand name Sonata) is a sedative/hypnotic mainly used for insomnia. It is a nonbenzodiazepine hypnotic from the pyrazolopyrimidine class. Elie, R., Rüther, E., Farr, I., Emilien, G., and Salinas, E. *Sleep la-*

tency is shortened during 4 weeks of treatment with zaleplon, a novel nonbenzodiazepine hypnotic. Zaleplon Clinical Study Group. J Clin Psychiatry: 536–44 (Aug 1999) Zaleplon is one of few sleep medications which have been found to not cause an increase in road traffic accidents, thus demonstrating a much higher safety profile than many other hypnotics currently on the market. Menzin, J., Lang, K.M., Levy, P., and Levy, E. *A general model of the effects of sleep medications on the risk and cost of motor vehicle accidents and its application to France.* Pharmacoeconomics 19 (1): 69–78 (January 2001); Vermeeren, A., Riedel, W.J., van Boxtel, M.P., Darwish, M., Paty, I., and Patat, A. *Differential residual effects of zaleplon and zopiclone on actual driving: a comparison with a low dose of alcohol.* Sleep Med. 25 (2): 224–31 (March 2002)

The side effects of Sonata are similar to the side effects of benzodiazepines, and its use may cause hallucinations, abnormal behavior, severe confusion, day-time drowsiness, dizziness or lightheadedness, unsteadiness and/or falls, double vision or other vision problems, agitation, headache, nausea, vomiting, diarrhea or abdominal pain, depression, muscle weakness, tremor, vivid or abnormal dreams and memory difficulties or amnesia. Sonata is habit-forming, meaning addiction or drug dependence may occur.

Zolpidem (Ambien)

Zolpidem, or known popularly as Ambien, is a prescription medication used for the short-term treatment of insomnia, as well as some brain disorders. Some users have reported unexplained sleepwalking while using Ambien, and a few have reported driving, binge eating, sleep talking, and performing other daily tasks while sleeping.

Driving while under the drug's influence is generally considered far more dangerous than the average impaired driver due to the diminished motor controls and delusions that may affect the driver. Residual 'hangover' effects such as sleepiness, impaired psychomotor skills may persist into the next day which may impair the ability of users to drive safely. Vermeeren A. *Residual effects of hypnotics: epidemiology and clinical implications*. CNS drugs. 18 (5): 297–328 (2004)

Studies suggest that the use of Ambien may impair driving skills with a resultant increased risk of road traffic accidents. Gustavsen, I., Bramness, J.G., Skurtveit, S., Engeland, A., Neutel, I., and Mørland, J. *Road traffic accident risk related to prescriptions of the hypnotics zopiclone, zolpidem, flunitrazepam and nitrazepam*. Sleep Med. 9 (8): 818–22 (December 2008)

The effects observed after having consumed Ambien are sleep induction, drowsiness, dizziness, lightheadedness, amnesia, confusion, concentration difficulties, and memory impairment. Couper, Fiona J., and Logan, Barry K. *Drugs and Human Performance Fact Sheets*. NHTSA. Page 93 (March 2004)

In the DUI context as it relates to field sobriety testing, horizontal gaze nystagmus, vertical gaze nystagmus (for high doses) and lack of convergence are present. Pupil size is normal and reaction to light is slow. *Id.* Pulse rate and blood pressure are down while body temperature is normal. Other characteristic indicators may include slow and slurred speech, and generally poor performance on field sobriety tests.

Carisoprodol (Meprobamate)

Carisoprodol is a centrally-acting skeletal muscle relaxant whose active metabolite is meprobamate. Carisoprodol is marketed in the United States under the brand name Soma, and in the United Kingdom and other countries under the brand names Sanoma and Carisoma. The brand name Soma is shared with the Soma/Haoma of ancient India, a drug mentioned in ancient Sanskrit writings and is also the name of the fictional drug featured in Aldous Huxley's Brave New World. *Brave New Soma. Time Magazine.* (June 08, 1959) Soma is also the Greek word for "body."

The effects observed after consuming carisoprodol include dizziness, drowsiness, sedation, confusion, disorientation, slowed thinking, lack of comprehension, drunken behavior, obtunded, coma. Couper, Fiona J., and Logan, Barry K. *Drugs and Human Performance Fact Sheets.* NHTSA. Page 15 (March 2004)

In the DUI context relating to field sobriety testing, horizontal gaze nystagmus, vertical gaze nystagmus (in high doses) and lack of convergence are present. Pupil size is normal to dilated and reaction to light is slow. Pulse rate, blood pressure, and body temperature are normal to lower. Other characteristic indicators may include slurred speech, drowsiness, disorientation, drunken behavior without the odor of alcohol, and generally poor performance on field sobriety tests.

Dextromethorphan (DXM or DM)

Dextromethorphan (DXM or DM) is an antitussive drug and is one of the active ingredients used to prevent coughs in many over-the-counter cold and cough medicines. Dextromethorphan has also found other uses in medicine, ranging from pain relief to psychological applications. It is sold in syrup, tablet, and lozenge forms manufactured under several different brand names and generic labels. In its pure form, dextromethorphan occurs as a white powder.

The observed effects after consumption of DXM at rec-ommended doses is minimal, although at higher recreational doses effects may include acute euphoria, elevated mood, dissociation of mind from body, creative dream-like experi-ences, and increased perceptual awareness. Other effects include disorientation, confusion, pupil dilation, and altered time perception, visual and auditory hallucinations, and de-creased sexual functioning. Couper, Fiona J., and Logan, Barry K. *Drugs and Human Performance Fact Sheets*. NHTSA. Page 35 (March 2004)

In the DUI context relating to field sobriety testing, hori-zontal gaze nystagmus, vertical gaze nystagmus (at high doses), and lack of convergence are present. Pupil size is nor-mal to dilated and reaction to light is slow. Pulse rate and blood pressure are down and body temperature is normal.

Diphenhydramine (Benadryl)

Diphenhydramine hydrochloride is a chemical mainly used as an antihistamine, antiemetic, sedative, and hypnotic. It is produced and marketed under the trade name Benadryl by McNeil-PPC (a division of Johnson & Johnson) in the U.S. & Canada, and Dimedrol in other countries. It is also found in the name-brand products Nytol and Unisom, though some Unisom products contain doxylamine instead.

Diphenhydramine was one of the first known antihistamines and was invented in 1943 by Dr. George Rieveschl, a former professor at the University of Cincinnati. Hevesi, D. *George Rieveschl, 91, Allergy Reliever, Dies*. New York Times. (September 29, 2007) It became the first FDA-approved prescription anti-histamine in 1946. Ritchie, J. *UC prof, Benadryl inventor dies*. Business Courier of Cincinnati. (September 24, 2007)

The observed effects of having consumed diphenhydramine may result in marked sedation, including drowsiness, reduced wakefulness, altered mood, impaired cognitive and psychomotor performance. Couper, Fiona J., and Logan, Barry K. *Drugs and Human Performance Fact Sheets*. NHTSA. Page 35 (March 2004)

In the DUI context relating to field sobriety testing, horizontal gaze nystagmus, vertical gaze nystagmus (at high doses), and lack of convergence are present. Pupil size is normal, dilatation may occur and reaction to light is slow. Pulse rate, blood pressure, and body temperature are normal. *Id.*

When this drug is mixed with alcohol the effects become more intense and therefore will likely cause increased impairment. Seppala, T., Linnoila, M, and Mattila, M.J. *Drugs, Alcohol and Driving*. Drugs. 17:389-408 (1979)

Ketamine

Ketamine is a drug used in human and veterinary medicine and was developed by Dr. Craig Newlands of Wayne State University. It was then further developed by Parke-Davis (today a part of Pfizer) in 1962 as part of an effort to find a safer anesthetic alternative to phencyclidine (PCP), which was more likely to cause hallucinations, neurotoxicity and seizures. The drug was first given to American soldiers during the Vietnam War.

The observed effects after having consumed ketamine includes decreased awareness of general environment, sedation, dream-like state, vivid dreams, feelings of invulnerability, increased distractibility, disorientation, and subjects are generally uncommunicative. Delirium and hallucinations can be experienced after awakening from anesthesia. Couper, Fiona

J., and Logan, Barry K. *Drugs and Human Performance Fact Sheets*. NHTSA. Page 45 (March 2004)

In the DUI context relating to field sobriety testing, horizontal gaze nystagmus, vertical gaze nystagmus, and lack of convergence are present. Pupil size and reaction to light are normal while pulse rate, blood pressure, and body temperature are elevated. *Id.*

Phencyclidine (PCP)

Phencyclidine (full name is phenylcyclohexylpiperidine but is commonly initialized as PCP), also known as angel dust and other street names, is a dissociative drug formerly used as an anesthetic agent. Maisto, Stephen A., Galizio, Mark and Connors, Gerard Joseph. *Drug Use and Abuse*. Thompson Wadsworth. (2004) PCP was first synthesized in 1926 and later tested after World War II as a surgical anesthetic.

The observed effects after consuming PCP include euphoria, calmness, feelings of strength and invulnerability, lethargy, disorientation, loss of coordination, distinct changes in body awareness, distorted sensory perceptions, impaired concentration, disordered thinking, illusions and hallucinations, agitation, combativeness or violence, memory loss, bizarre behavior, sedation, and stupor. Couper, Fiona J., and Logan, Barry K. *Drugs and Human Performance Fact Sheets*. NHTSA. Page 79 (March 2004)

In the DUI context relating to field sobriety testing, horizontal gaze nystagmus, vertical gaze nystagmus, and lack of convergence are present. Pupil size and reaction to light are normal, which pulse rate, blood pressure, and body temperature are elevated. *Id.*

Toluene

Toluene, also known as methylbenzene, phenylmethane, and Toluol, is a clear water-insoluble liquid with the typical smell of paint thinners, redolent of the sweet smell of the related compound benzene. Toluene is a common solvent, able to dissolve paints, paint thinners, silicone sealants, many chemical reactants, rubber, printing ink, adhesives (glues), lacquers, leather tanners, and disinfectants.

The observed effects after consuming dizziness, euphoria, grandiosity, floating sensation, drowsiness, reduced ability to concentrate, slowed reaction time, distorted perception of time and distance, confusion, weakness, fatigue, memory loss, delusions, and hallucinations. Couper, Fiona J., and Logan, Barry K. *Drugs and Human Performance Fact Sheets.* NHTSA. Page 85 (March 2004)

In the DUI context relating to field sobriety testing, horizontal gaze nystagmus (in high doses), vertical gaze nystagmus (in high doses), and lack of convergence are present. Pupil size is normal and reaction to light is slow. Pulse rate and blood pressure are elevated while body temperature is normal. *Id.*

CHAPTER 11

Choosing an Attorney

If you have been charged with a DUI, your first priority should be finding a good attorney. In fact, if you appear at an arraignment (your first court appearance) without an attorney, most Judges will highly recommend that you hire an attorney to represent you. Today's DUI laws are extraordinarily complicated and the punishment is potentially severe so you need an attorney who is experienced and who has dedicated most of his or her practice to defending those accused of DUIs. While there is no easy formula for determining if any one attorney is better than another, there are certain criteria that you should consider in your search. Ultimately the search must be for the attorney who will get you the best result possible.

What a qualified DUI attorney will give you is a reasonable chance at getting a good deal. If there is a legal defense a good DUI attorney will find it and exploit it. DUI attorneys are trained at spotting issues and finding legal defenses. Additionally, good DUI attorneys will immediately garner the attention of the prosecutor. Many prosecutors will give established DUI attorneys the benefit of the doubt and give their clients fair offers strictly based on reputation. This is an advantage that every defendant should have.

So, where do you begin? The problem with finding a good DUI attorney is that the vast majority of DUI defendants are first time offenders (which is good) who have never had to have a DUI attorney before. The best way to find a competent attorney is by asking another attorney (who is not a DUI attorney). A referral from another attorney should ensure some certainty that the DUI attorney is competent and well thought of. The other sources in your search would be friends or acquaintances who have been charged with a DUI. Finally, the way most locate a DUI attorney is by traditional advertising (yellow pages or facsimile) or the internet. Of these two forums (yellow pages and internet), it is my opinion that by the more valuable of the two is the internet. The internet is a wonderful tool and permits the defendant to more thoroughly research the attorney and their credentials. However, one must proceed with caution when using the internet because as wonderful as it is, it can make an attorney appear greater than what he or she really is. That being said, you are able to learn about the attorney's experience, area of expertise, the staff the attorney has working for him, his training, and his general thoroughness.

Besides the research you do when preparing for hiring an attorney, the next most valuable thing is to talk to and personally meet with the attorney. This way you can ask your pertinent questions and see what the response is from the attorney to your questions. At such a meeting you and the attorney should discuss your case in detail, the DUI laws and how they apply in your case, possible defenses and outcomes, the prosecuting attorney in your case and how they deal with DUIs, and the cost of representation. If any of these topics are not discussed to your satisfaction do not hire the attorney.

First and foremost the attorney must have the experience and competence to ably represent you in court. While there is never a guarantee of a successful outcome, an experienced and competent attorney will give you a fighting chance at a good result. Once you are satisfied that the attorney has the necessary qualifications you must decide if you feel comfortable working with him; essentially, you must be certain that he has a good "bedside manner." If you do not feel comfortable with the attorney or feel that his personality does not mesh with yours, then keep searching. You have too much to lose and you must be comfortable with your decision. You will be relying on your attorney to represent your best interests to the prosecuting attorney and fight for you in court. You must feel like he is the best attorney for you.

The following are important considerations when looking for the right attorney to represent you in your DUI case.

DUI Experience

If you have been charged with a DUI and are facing issues like a conviction, a license suspension, and jail, you do not want to be represented by an attorney who has limited experienced. Let him get his experience at someone else's expense or at the prosecuting attorney or public defender's office. The fact is that DUIs are complicated and have many more issues than most criminal matters. Unless the attorney has encountered all of these potential issues and dealt with different prosecuting attorneys and Judges, they will not be equipped to handle your case.

So, how much experience is necessary? A good DUI attorney has handled at least hundreds of DUI cases in different jurisdictions for many years. Be certain of their experience before you retain the attorney. If you want to confirm when the attorney was admitted to practice law, check with the State's Bar Association.

DUI Emphasis

Regardless of the attorney's experience, the number of years practicing law is irrelevant if the attorney's practice does not emphasize DUI law. DUI law is not static and requires the attorney to be constantly involved and active in the practice. A lawyer who dedicates only a small percentage of his practice to the practice of DUIs cannot keep up to date with the ever changing practice and cannot represent your rights as well as an attorney who dedicates himself primarily to DUI practice. On more than one occasion I have received a call from an attorney with more years of practice than myself who is asking me my opinion on a particular DUI issue because they do not practice DUI law very often. You are going to pay good money for legal representation, be should you get the best value for your dollar and the best value is only represented by an attorney who specializes in DUI law.

DUI Education

The attorney you hire must also be well educated in DUI laws. To that end, be certain that your DUI attorney has completed continuing education classes and seminars in DUI law. These classes are offered by State and County Bar Associations, criminal defense organizations, and private organizations focusing on DUI education (ie. National College for DUI Defense). Such classes focus on updated case law, new legal challenges to the statutes governing DUIs and breath test machinery, and field sobriety tests, to name just some of the areas that updates and continued education assist the DUI attorney.

Familiarity with Courts

One of the more important factors when retaining an attorney is determining whether that attorney is familiar with the court and Judge where your DUI is to be prosecuted. The reason that this is important is because each court deals with DUIs differently. For example, the Judge in a particular court might demand that prior to any plea you have completed an alcohol evaluation while other Judge's will allow some latitude. Additionally, the Judge in one court may be tougher on DUIs than a Judge in another court and may not always follow a plea agreement. If this is known in advance then your attorney may have you do additional work, such as community service, prior to a plea so that the likelihood of a tougher sentence is minimized. The difference in courts and their practices and procedures are many and the more knowledgeable your attorney is the better the possibility of an outcome and the more likely your rights will be protected.

Familiarity with Prosecuting Attorneys

The reality is that if your attorney is familiar with the prosecuting attorney and on friendly terms, the more likely you will receive a more favorable result. There is no real science to this except to say that if a prosecuting attorney has a history with your attorney which involves tough but fair dealing, the prosecuting attorney will likely deal with your attorney in a more direct and less severe manner. In most instances this happens as a matter of course. This does not necessarily mean that your attorney will be able to construct an improbable deal just because he knows the prosecutor, however, it does mean that in many instances if a prosecuting attorney is considering a possible amendment to a lesser offense, it is more likely your attorney will procure such a deal while another attorney may not.

Reputation

Reputation is king in this business. However, how does one learn of an attorney's reputation? That's a tough question to answer. Those in the know, prosecuting attorneys, Judges, and fellow attorneys, are not readily accessible to defendants inquiring about a DUI attorney. However, if you do have access to a non-DUI attorney it is worth inquiring what their opinion is regarding a top DUI attorney. Besides asking another attorney for a referral, one of the best resources would be individuals who have been previously charged with a DUI. If you know such an individual ask them who represented them and their opinion. If you are attending alcohol treatment or AA meetings, ask fellow attendees and see who represented them and what they thought of the representation.

Staff

You will find that that majority of DUI attorneys are solo practitioners. I am of the opinion that solo practitioners or smaller law firms do better jobs with DUIs than large faceless law firms. DUIs are not cases that should be handed off to associate attorneys or given to legal secretaries to work on. That may sound ludicrous, but it happens a great deal. Be sure that the attorney you hire is the attorney who will actually work on the case. Be insistent on this and if it does not happen, walk away before you hire the attorney. Another important consideration is the support staff. Are they familiar with DUIs and do they have experience working with DUIs and the Department of Licensing? If not, move on. Again, the devil is in the details and a good assistant can make the difference between, for example, keeping or losing your license.

Personality

The personality of your attorney should be something you are comfortable with. This is very much a personal thing but if you find your attorney to be grumpy, non-communicative, and distant, it may be difficult for you to keep the relationship civil during the many months you will be together. Ultimately this is a personal decision but think with your head and your heart. If you do not feel that the relationship will work, move on. Trust your instincts.

Cost

Cost is a tricky subject when it comes to DUI lawyers. There are some DUI lawyers who have extraordinarily high overhead costs and much of the fees are to cover rent, advertising, staff, and so on. Some of these attorneys may well be worth the cost while many others are not. If you like the wood paneled offices with a view and a personally made latte to your specifications, feel free to employ the most expensive attorneys. However, the cost of the attorney is rarely a barometer of that attorney's reputation and success.

While the above is true, properly defending DUI cases

does take an extraordinary amount of time and effort. Those attorneys who expend the appropriate effort are typically more expensive because they charge a certain amount based on the estimated number of hours they will spend on your case. Hence, avoid the cheapest attorneys as they are likely charging less money due to fewer hours working on your case, less experience, and less DUI specific training (which is expensive but necessary to properly defend DUI cases).

Most attorneys will charge "flat fees," which is a one-time all-inclusive fee. Although this flat fee seems gargantuan at the beginning of the case, if it is all inclusive you will not be surprised by hidden costs along the way. Most attorneys will allow you to pay the flat fee in a number of payments. Do not shy away from asking the attorney their costs and how this compares to other attorneys in their area. Finally, for your own protection be sure to receive, review, and sign an attorney-client agreement (contract).

CHAPTER 12

Miscellaneous DUI Issues

Travel to Canada

<u>Inadmissible Entry into Canada</u>

If you travel to Canada and are facing a criminal charge, whether it be a more serious felony matter or a "simple" misdemeanor, you must know the implications of a conviction. The Canadian Government has determined that certain persons are "inadmissible" to Canada and therefore are not allowed to enter Canada or remain in Canada. Members of Inadmissible Classes include those persons who have been convicted of certain criminal offenses, which include, but are not limited to:

- Felony convictions
- Possession of illegal substances
- Unauthorized possession of a firearm
- Shoplifting
- Theft
- Assault

The Canadian Government also views a DUI as an extremely serious offense. If you are convicted of a DUI you will not be permitted entry into Canada. That being said, if you wish to travel to Canada there is a means to either remove the status of "inadmissible" or travel into the country while you are "inadmissible" if you follow certain procedures. Click on *www.washdui.com* and go to "important links" for the Government of Canada website for more information and the application.

Inadmissible Status Removal

You can remove the "Inadmissibility Status" by applying for a Minister's Approval of Rehabilitation. You may initiate this process five years after the end of probation.

Entering Canada with an Inadmissible Status

If necessary you may enter Canada during the Inadmissible Status. To do so you must apply for a Temporary Resident Permit. If you are seeking entry for a single or limited period the Temporary Resident Permit application must be completed and the Canadian Government will charge a fee for the Temporary Resident Permit.

Immigration Consequences

For those who are not U.S. Citizens there are bigger consequences that result from a DUI conviction than jail, fines, and a license suspension. Depending on the specific State statutes DUI convictions can be determined to be a "crime involving moral turpitude" and a "crime of violence" under present US immigration laws. Such a conviction can lead to inadmissibility to or deportation from the U.S., denial of adjustment during the green card process, or a finding of bad moral character at a naturalization interview. *If you are not a U.S. citizen you should immediately consult with an immigration attorney.*

Crime Involving Moral Turpitude (CIMT)

Under the U.S. immigration laws, a "crime involving moral turpitude" (or the admission of the acts that constitute such a crime) is grounds for inadmissibility to the United States and can result in deportation from the United States.

Generally, in order to involve "moral turpitude," a crime must have an intent requirement. Obvious examples would include murder and theft, for instance. In contrast, certain other crimes do not have an intent requirement and one such example, as defined in most State laws, is a DUI which contains no reference to intent. That means, one does not have to have intended to get the car and drive under the influence.

As a result a DUI conviction is not considered a CIMT unless it is combined with an aggravating factor. It is important to note that while a DUI conviction alone will not result in a denial of an immigration benefit, lying about it on one's application can and would bring up a fraud or misrepresentation charge and can create a permanent bar to reentry, often without waiver possibilities.

Crime of Violence

As stated, even if the DUI conviction does not involve a crime involving moral turpitude, it could still have serious immigration consequences if that conviction is determined to be an "aggravated felony". Aggravated felonies, generally violent or other specified crimes for which the wrongdoer can be sentenced for one year or more, can lead to removal.

Citizenship

In the event that a non-resident is able to avoid inadmissibility or removal resulting from a DUI conviction, even one such conviction still can affect the alien's naturalization process. The U.S. Citizenship and Immigration Services (USCIS) may consider any criminal conviction in making a determination regarding good moral character for purposes of an application for naturalization.

It is imperative to be honest when considering naturalization and disclose all previous arrests and convictions with an immigration attorney before applying for citizenship. Although one DUI would not automatically disqualify the applicant, one must disclose it and have completed the probation before filing a citizenship application. Also, several DUI convictions can render the applicant a habitual drunkard and result in inadmissibility, and even removal.

Car Rentals

A DUI conviction may prevent you from renting a vehicle from a commercial agency. The policies of rental companies vary and you should consult different companies. For instance, some rental companies will rent to individuals who have been convicted of a DUI, but charge the individual a higher rental rate. The problem is even greater if you have been ordered not to drive unless you have installed an ignition interlock device. Additionally, if you have a restrictive license (such as an Ignition Interlock license of an Occupational License) rental agencies may not honor such a license.

Vacating a DUI Conviction (Expungement)

Many states do permit a person to vacate (expunge) a DUI while alternatively, many states do not. You must check with an attorney in your state of origin whether the DUI conviction (or other conviction) can be vacated and/or sealed.

Sobriety Checkpoints/Check Stops

One of the limited exceptions to the requirements of probable cause to stop a vehicle (the *Terry* stop) is the sobriety checkpoint. If a driver is stopped at a sobriety checkpoint in a State that permits them, no probable cause to validate such an intrusion is required.

Sobriety checkpoints, roadblocks, check stops, as they are collectively called depending on jurisdiction, involve law enforcement officials positioning themselves on a road way and stopping every vehicle, or random vehicles and investigating the possibility that the driver is under the influence of alcohol or drugs. Such check points are established late at night or in the very early morning hours, typically on weekends which is when a higher percentage of impaired drivers tend to be on the road.

The officer's task after contact with the driver is to determine whether the driver has consumed alcohol or drugs and if so whether there is suspicion of being under the influence of these substances. If the officer suspects the driver is possibly under the influence the driver will be asked to exit the vehicle and take voluntary field sobriety tests. If the driver's performance on these tests is poor he will then be required take an alcohol breath test.

The legality of such checkpoints has been in question in the United States for some time. In these scenarios drivers are stopped and contacted without reasonable suspicion and may be tested summarily and without probable cause.

The Fourth Amendment to the United States Constitution states that:

> The right of the people to be secure in their persons, houses, papers, and effects, against unreasonable searches and seizures, shall not be violated, and no Warrants shall issue, but upon probable cause, supported by Oath or affirmation, and particularly describing the place to be searched, and the persons or things to be seized.

On its face the United States Constitution appears to prohibit drivers from being stopped without a search warrant or probable cause that they have committed a criminal offense (or violated the law). The United States Supreme Court was asked to rule on this very issue in 1990 with the case *Michigan Dept. of State Police v. Sitz*, 496 U.S. 444 (1990).

The United States Supreme Court found that properly conducted sobriety checkpoints were constitutional while also concluding that such checkpoints did in fact infringe on a constitutional right. Former Chief Justice Rehnquist argued that the state interest in reducing drunk driving outweighed this infringement. *Id.* He further stated that sobriety roadblocks were effective and necessary. *Id.*

Despite the Unites States Supreme Court ruling not all states have agreed that sobriety checkpoints are constitutionally valid. In fact ten states have found that sobriety roadblocks violate their own state constitutions or have outlawed them

(Idaho, Iowa, Michigan, Minnesota, Oregon, Rhode Island, Texas, Washington, Wisconsin, and Wyoming).

Employment Consequences

A DUI arrest may prove devastating on your employment status. If you need to drive to work and your license has been suspended this may severely compromise your position. Of perhaps bigger concern is what will happen, if anything, if your employer finds out you have been charged (or convicted) of a DUI.

Private Employers (that are not health care facilities, schools, financial institutions, and other "special" employers) do not have the right to request your entire criminal history. In fact, unauthorized use of your private information is a crime. In particular, most private employers do not have a right to certain information and cannot use them in hiring decisions. Such information includes arrests that did not lead to a conviction or participation in a pretrial diversion program which was successfully completed. If an employer somehow learns of your arrest record, the Labor Code prohibits him or her from considering any arrest that did not lead to a conviction, or any arrest that led to a diversion program, in making decisions regarding hiring, firing or promotion. However, because criminal arrests, prosecutions, and convictions are public records, private employers sometimes hire private investigation firms to conduct background checks on all applicants and/or all employees. These background checks can uncover all public records, including "expunged" and/or dismissed convictions.

When considering how to address the issue of a prior criminal history with an employer or potential employer, take into account the law regarding criminal records and private employers. Remember that you have the right not to disclose juvenile records, "expunged" records, otherwise dismissed records (i.e., dismissed upon successful completion of diversion program), or records of arrests not leading to convictions. If your conviction has been dismissed or "expunged," you have a right to answer "no" if you are asked if you have been convicted of a crime. However, when in doubt it is critical to discuss this issue with your attorney.

The matter of disclosure is a little different when it comes to "special employers," which would include schools, healthcare facilities, eldercare facilities, childcare facilities, and financial institutions. The law allows for certain types of employers to have access to your entire criminal history to determine employment. Generally, these employers serve people who are considered vulnerable (i.e., children, sick, elderly) or they handle sensitive matters (i.e., financial institutions, public utilities, nuclear facilities, pharmacies, etc.). To have access under this exception, the law requires that: (1) the employer must have explicit authorization under the law to see summary criminal history information, (2) disclosure relates to specific criminal conduct (i.e., specific crimes, not just any convictions), and (3) that employers act on the existence of such information. For example, the law might require the exclusion of job applicants with certain convictions, like a DUI, from certain jobs, such as a pilot or school bus driver. Examples would include employment that requires licensing and certification, such as real estate brokers, doctors, nurses, attorneys, etc.

Government and public employers may see summary criminal histories in considering an application for a job if authorized by law. Essentially, any government jobs for which a background check is required have the authority to check your criminal history.

If you are applying for a law enforcement job, you must list all arrests, including those that did not result in a conviction, as well as traffic summonses. If the application allows you to eliminate some cases, such as those that resulted in a traffic infraction only, or the employer is interested in knowing only about convictions within a certain number of years, then you may properly disclose only the information requested.

DUI and a Pilot License

Clearly, anyone with a pilot license should not even consider drinking and driving. The Federal Aviation Administration (FAA) strictly enforces the regulation of alcohol and those licensed to fly. It is the responsibility of the pilot to report certain conduct for the Airman Medical Certificate. If a pilot declines to disclose certain conduct on their Airman Medical Certificate, they can be assured the FAA will impose severe sanctions.

The Pilot Records Improvement Act of 1996 requires an air carrier, before hiring an individual as a pilot, to request, with the individual's written consent, the Chief Driver licensing official of a state to perform a National Driver Register (NDR) file check. Information on the NDR file that was reported by the states during the past 5-years and any withdrawal action still in effect will be disclosed.

Vehicle Impound

Another penalty or sanction that many states have at their disposal is to impound the vehicle of the DUI offender. Eleven

States have laws permitting impoundment for DUI related offenses (AK, CA, CT, FL, IA, KS, MO, MS, OR, VA, WA) and this does not include state laws where the impoundment is temporary (hours) to prevent impaired offenders from driving after release from arrest. Fell, James C., Voas, Robert B., McKnight, A. Scott, and Levy, Marvin. *A National Survey of Vehicle Sanction Laws for Alcohol-Related Driving Offenses in the United States: Preliminary Findings.* Pacific Institute for Research & Evaluation, Calverton, MD National Highway Traffic Safety Administration, Washington, DC. Seattle, Wa. (2007)

Vehicle Immobilization

Another tool to prevent DUI offenders from using their vehicle is immobilizing their vehicle. This is done by using a bar-type locking device ("club") on the steering wheel or locking device on a wheel ("boot"). Thirteen States have laws permitting vehicle immobilization as a sanction for impaired driving offenses (FL, IA, IL, KS, MI, MS, NM, OH, OR, SC, VA, VT, WI). Fell, James C., Voas, Robert B., McKnight, A. Scott, and Levy, Marvin. *A National Survey of Vehicle Sanction Laws for Alcohol-Related Driving Offenses in the United States: Preliminary Findings.* Pacific Institute for Research & Evaluation, Calverton, MD National Highway Traffic Safety Administration, Washington, DC. Seattle, Wa. (2007)

Special License Plates or Plate Markings

This sanction includes placing special markings or designations on the license plate that alert police that a convicted DUI offender is in a family or group that drives that vehicle.

The special license plate or plate marking sanction permits other family members access to the vehicle, but prohibits the convicted offender from driving it. Six States have laws permitting special license plates for impaired driving offenses (GA, HI, MI, MN, NJ, OH). Fell, James C., Voas, Robert B., McKnight, A. Scott, and Levy, Marvin. *A National Survey of Vehicle Sanction Laws for Alcohol-Related Driving Offenses in the United States: Preliminary Findings.* Pacific Institute for Research & Evaluation, Calverton, MD National Highway Traffic Safety Administration, Washington, DC. Seattle, Wa. (2007)

The Emotional Struggle

The "Five Stages of Grief"

Being arrested for a DUI can be a monumentally difficult event to deal with. The initial shock of the arrest may take many weeks, or longer, to get over. However, those who have been charged with DUI find many other troubling obstacles that they must face over the course of litigation in the court system, and beyond. These "obstacles" may be substantive, like license suspensions and perhaps loss of employment, or emotional issues dealing with the guilt and perhaps self inflicted shame of being labeled a "criminal." And while it is true that everyone deals with the emotional issues of such a situation differently it has been observed that many have similar emotional patterns when dealing with the reality of being charged with driving under the influence.

The emotional trauma and eventual scarring that may occur is rarely if ever talked about between clients and their attorneys. Further, I have researched this issue in the realm of DUIs and there is little written about the subject. This is unfortunate as it is definitely an issue that must be dealt with by every person dealing with a DUI arrest and charge.

Over the course of many years of practice I have continually seen clients on an emotional pendulum. Seemingly many are angry one minute and remorseful the next. This is normal. However, my wife Janean, who also works in the DUI field and has for many years, has cleverly analyzed the emotional turmoil our clients go through and has likened it to the five stages of grief. The five stages of grief, or as used in the current context, the five stages of dealing with a DUI, include denial, anger, bargaining, depression, and acceptance.

The five stages of grief, technically known as the Kübler-Ross model, was first introduced by Elisabeth Kübler-Ross in her 1969 book, *On Death and Dying*. Kübler-Ross, E. *On Death and Dying*. Routledge. (1973) This book first described 5 discrete stages with which people deal with grief and tragedy, especially when diagnosed with a terminal illness or catastrophic loss. However, she also used these five stages for people suffering from any form of catastrophic personal loss (job, income, freedom). This may also include significant life events such as the death of a loved one, divorce, drug addiction, the onset of a disease or chronic illness, an infertility diagnosis, as well many tragedies and disasters. This is where the analysis seems to fit well in the context of those individuals suffering from the consequences of the original DUI charge and all of the subsequent collateral consequences.

The progression of the five stages of grief is:

1. Denial – Denial is usually only a temporary defense for the individual. This feeling is generally replaced with heightened awareness of positions and individuals that will be left behind after death.

2. Anger – Once in the second stage, the individual recognizes that denial cannot continue. Because of anger, the person is very difficult to care for due to misplaced feelings of rage and envy.

3. Bargaining – The third stage involves the hope that the individual can somehow postpone or delay reality – whatever reality may be given their specific facts of a DUI case. In the DUI context this is often manifested directly to me, the attorney, with questions such as; "If I pay more money will the prosecutor reduce my DUI?"; "Will the Judge not send me to jail if he knows that I am a good citizen and contribute to society?"

4. Depression – During the fourth stage, the defendant begins to understand the certainty of what the DUI will result in, whether it be a driving license suspension, jail, or even a reduced charge (which still may carry with it significant collateral consequences).

5. Acceptance – In this last stage, the individual begins to come to terms with his situation or that of his loved one.

The original author, Kübler-Ross, claimed these steps do not necessarily appear in the sequence noted above. Similarly not all steps are necessarily experienced by all individuals, though she stated a person will always experience at least two. She noted that people will often experience several stages in a "roller coaster" effect—switching between two or more stages, returning to one or more several times before working through it.

If you find yourself suffering through one of these emotional stages be aware that the stages will be worked through and the ultimate stage of "acceptance" will eventually be reached. In other words, things will inevitably get better. If you are suffering and feel the need to deal with your emotions professionally, please talk to your attorney or treatment provider for advice. Your emotional needs must be dealt with so please do not ignore them.

CHAPTER 13

Washington State Statutes/Case Law

[<.15/>.15 or Refusal]	1st DUI	2nd DUI	3rd DUI
Jail	1 day/2 days	30 days/45 days	90 days/120 days
EHM		60 days /90 days	120 days/150 days
Fine	$866/$1121	$1121/$1503	$1928/$2778
License Suspension	90 days/1 year	2 year s/3 years	3 years/4 years
SR 22 Insurance	3 years	3 years	3 years
Ignition Interlock	1 year	1-5 years	1-10 years
Alcohol/Drug Eval	Yes	Yes	Yes
DUI Victim's Panel	Yes	Yes	Yes
Probation	5 years	5 years	5 years

Driving Under the Influence (DUI)

RCW 46.61.502

Unfortunately we cannot avoid looking at the statute for the explanation of a DUI. This is the case because a DUI is the creation of the Legislature who defines the crime in the form of a statute. As a result, it is the statute in each state that defines what a DUI is and it is this definition that the prosecutor must prove beyond a reasonable doubt.

In Washington State a person is guilty of driving while under the influence of intoxicating liquor or any drug if the person drives a vehicle within the state:

> (a) And the person has, within two hours after driving, an alcohol concentration of 0.08 or higher as shown by analysis of the person's breath or blood made under RCW 46.61.506; or
>
> (b) While the person is under the influence of or affected by intoxicating liquor or any drug; or
>
> (c) While the person is under the combined influence of or affected by intoxicating liquor and any drug.

Looking at the statute it is clear that it is not only the excessive consumption of alcohol that can place the driver in fear of being arrested for a DUI, but also the use of drugs, legal or illegal, that can put in criminal jeopardy a driver of a motor vehicle. Further, lawful use of a prescription drug is not a defense to a charge of DUI.

Physical Control

RCW 46.61.504

The law states that you are in physical control of a motor vehicle if you are in a position to physically operate and control a motor vehicle. You do not need to be moving the car or even have moved the car to be properly charged with the offense. Over the years this law has been somewhat refined and now there is a requirement that you not only be in a position to physically operate a motor vehicle but also have the means to do so. Typically this involves having the ignition keys in close proximity or in the ignition switch.

The statute for Physical Control, RCW 46.61.504, reads as follows:

(1) A person is guilty of being in actual physical control of a motor vehicle while under the influence of intoxicating liquor or any drug if the person has actual physical control of a vehicle within this state:

  (a) And the person has, within two hours after being in actual physical control of the vehicle, an alcohol concentration of 0.08 or higher as shown by analysis of the person's breath or blood made under RCW 46.61.506; or

  (b) While the person is under the influence of or affected by intoxicating liquor or any drug; or

  (c) While the person is under the combined influence of or affected by intoxicating liquor and any drug.

The statute for this offense is not very helpful in defining the element of "physical control." However, case law helps to a degree as it is defines being in "actual physical control of a motor vehicle" as having the authority to manage a reasonably operable vehicle or is in a position to regulate movement of the vehicle. *State v. Smelter*, 36 Wn. App. 439, 674 P.2d 690 (1984).

In a practical setting, if you are "drunk" and in your car with the engine running to warm your vehicle while you sober up you have committed a crime. Therefore, even though you have made the correct decision not to drive, you can be charged with physical control. Sounds harsh and perhaps it is.

The statute does help in defining the defense to this crime. The statute states specifically that being "safely off the roadway" is a defense to the crime. A regular DUI is not afforded such a defense. *State v. Hazzard*, 43 Wn. App. 335, 717 P.2d 282 (1986), *State v. Beck*, 42 Wn. App. 12, 707 P.2d 1380 (1985), review denied, 105 Wn.2d 1004 (1986). Because this particular defense is so valuable there are many instances where officers actually charge a DUI rather than physical control to eliminate the possibility of this defense. To do so the driver must actually be seen driving prior to pulling off the roadway.

In utilizing the defense of safely off the roadway you must remember the definition of "roadway," as it is rather broad. "Roadway" is defined as "that portion of a highway improved, designed, or used for vehicular travel exclusive of the sidewalk or shoulder." RCW 46.04.600. Interestingly, a private parking lot may be considered a roadway, if there is a threat posed to the public. *Edmonds v. Ostby*, 48 Wn. App. 867, 740 P.2d 916, review denied, 109 Wn.2d 1016 (1987).

Juvenile DUI (Minor DUI)

RCW 46.61.503

Under Washington law, it is a crime for a person under the age of 21 to drive or to be in physical control of a vehicle after consuming alcohol with an alcohol concentration over 0.02. This is a strict standard and is treated with zero tolerance. The amount of alcohol required to get to a level of 0.02 is minimal, less than one beer or a glass of wine. Such a violation has grave consequences and may result in a criminal charge, an arrest, license suspension, and possibly jail.

The statute for a juvenile DUI, RCW 46.61.503, reads as follows:

(1) Notwithstanding any other provision of this title, a person is guilty of driving or being in physical control of a motor vehicle after consuming alcohol if the person operates or is in physical control of a motor vehicle within this state and the person:

(a) Is under the age of twenty-one;

(b) Has, within two hours after operating or being in physical control of the motor vehicle, an alcohol concentration of at least 0.02 but less than the concentration specified in RCW 46.61.502, as shown by analysis of the person's breath or blood made under RCW 46.61.506.

A "minor DUI" is a misdemeanor and has a maximum penalty of 90 days in jail and a $1,000 fine. Additionally, in all likelihood there will be probation for up to two years and the conditions imposed by the court at sentencing will certainly include an alcohol assessment and follow up (an 8 hour alcohol awareness class or lengthy alcohol treatment), the attendance at a DUI victim's panel, and possibly community service or jail time.

Additionally there is also the possibility of a 90 day license suspension imposed by the Department of Licensing for those arrested for a minor DUI. This suspension occurs irrespective of the outcome in the criminal case.

Finally, if you are a minor and have a breath rest result of .08 or greater, or if the prosecutor can prove that you were impaired at the time of driving, you can also be prosecuted for an adult DUI and be facing the same consequences, including mandatory jail.

Boating Under the Influence (BUI)

RCW 79A.60.040

To the surprise of many there is something called "boating under the influence." Not only is it against the law but it is a criminal misdemeanor offense. In Washington, the actual offense is called "Operation of a Vessel Under the Influence of Intoxicating Liquor." The statute for a BUI, RCW 79A.60.040(2), reads as follows:

(2) It shall be a violation for a person to operate a vessel while under the influence of intoxicating liquor or any drug. A person is considered to be under the influence of intoxicating liquor or any drug if:

(a) The person has 0.08 grams or more of alcohol per two hundred ten liters of breath, as shown by analysis of the person's breath made under RCW 46.61.506; or

(b) The person has 0.08 percent or more by weight of alcohol in the person's blood, as shown by analysis of the person's blood made under RCW 46.61.506; or

(c) The person is under the influence of or affected by intoxicating liquor or any drug; or

(d) The person is under the combined influence of or affected by intoxicating liquor and any drug.

States, including Washington State, have enacted criminal laws that penalize certain conduct while operating a "vessel" on the water. A "vessel" includes almost every description of watercraft on the water, other than a seaplane, used or capable of being used as a means of transportation on the water. RCW 79A.60.010.

There are several important differences between a regular DUI and a BUI. These differences include the following:

- For a BUI, unlike a DUI, is a misdemeanor with a maximum punishment of 90 days in jail and a $1,000 fine.
- For a BUI, there are no mandatory minimum penalties while for a DUI the mandatory penalties include at least one day in jail (and fines) for a first offense and dramatically increase thereafter for multiple offenses.
- For a BUI there is no driver's license consequences. Therefore, unlike DUIs you cannot lose your license if you arrested for or convicted of a BUI.
- For a BUI there is no ignition interlock devise requirement. While a judge can always impose such a devise, unlike a DUI conviction it is not a mandatory requirement.
- For a BUI arrest you do not need to take a breath test or blood test, unlike if you arrested for a DUI. Therefore there will be no license suspension if you refuse to take a breath or blood test. If you are asked to take such a test by a law enforcement officer it would advised that you exercise your rights and politely decline to take it.
- For a BUI, there are no mandatory punishment enhancements for multiple offenses. However, a judge

would still have the discretion to increase punishment should he chose to do so.

Felony DUI

RCW 46.61.502

A charge of DUI or Physical Control is a felony if you have four or more prior offenses in the previous ten years. A "prior offense" is defined as a conviction for a DUI or Physical Control, successful completion of a deferred prosecution, or a conviction for Reckless Driving, Reckless Endangerment, or Negligent Driving 1st Degree, where the charge was initially filed as a DUI or Physical Control.

Additionally, a DUI or Physical Control charge is also a felony if you have a prior conviction for an alcohol related vehicular assault or vehicular homicide.

A DUI felony is classified as a level V felony and the sentencing range for such an offense is 22-29 months in prison. Although the felony DUI offense is a Class C felony it cannot be vacated from a person's criminal history after five years like many other Class C felonies. Instead you must wait ten years until this type of charge can be vacated from you criminal history.

Reducing the DUI Charge

The objective of any DUI attorney is to ensure that their client does not end up with a DUI on their record. Clearly the hope is that the DUI is dismissed and that all related charges disappear. While this does occur from time to time, the reality is that most cases with a qualified DUI attorney are disposed of with the amendment of the DUI charge to a lesser offense.

Equally as true is that occasionally DUI cases present very few defenses and have circumstances that do not lend themselves to an amendment and then the job of the attorney is to mitigate the damage that has already been done.

The facts of the DUI usually dictate what will ultimately happen with the charge. If you have a BAC reading of more than twice the limit and all available defenses cannot be successfully challenged, or all challenges have failed, the chance of having the DUI charge amended to a lesser offense becomes a difficult proposition. Further, if there is an accident or there are passengers in the vehicle who are minor children, it becomes an even more difficult proposition to have the DUI charges amended to a lesser offense. At times when all legal defenses have been challenged but have failed your attorney has to be adept at mitigating the damage. In other words, worst case scenario your attorney has to ensure that your DUI case doesn't go from bad to worse with the addition of greater penalties, including more jail. In cases with high BAC readings (over 0.15), when an amendment to a lesser offense is not an option, your attorney should at least be able to work an offer of "no BAC reading," which may help with a license suspension and will lower mandatory jail and fines.

Reckless Driving

RCW 46.61.500

Reckless driving is a crime in Washington State and is a "gross-misdemeanor" and punishable by up to 365 days in jail and a fine of $5000. Unlike DUIs there is no mandatory penalty sentence and therefore no mandatory jail. Another significant difference is that probation is 2 years in length, not 5 years as it is in a DUI. Lastly, reckless driving is a non-alcohol related crime.

If convicted of reckless driving there is an automatic license suspension of 30 days. This suspension will not take effect immediately but you will receive notice from the DOL after the court approves of the plea. The court then forwards the plea of Reckless Driving to the DOL and the DOL then issues the suspension. The suspension will result in the requirement of SR-22 insurance for 3 years.

If you are not a citizen of the United States you should be careful when considering a plea to Reckless Driving. While immigration laws are evolving and Reckless Driving no longer appears to equal an immediate deportation ticket, it still is dangerous territory so if you are not an American citizen be certain that you consult with an immigration attorney prior to accepting an offer of Reckless Driving.

The statutory definition of Reckless Driving is:

(1) Any person who drives any vehicle in willful or wanton disregard for the safety of persons or property is guilty of reckless driving. Violation of the provisions of this section is a gross misdemeanor punishable by imprisonment of not more than one year and by a fine of not more than five thousand dollars.

(2) The license or permit to drive or any nonresident privilege of any person convicted of reckless driving shall be suspended by the department for not less than thirty days.

Reckless Endangerment

RCW 9A.36.050

It is not uncommon to see the charge of Reckless

Endangerment charged along with a DUI or, have the threat of a charge of Reckless Endangerment being added to your DUI charge. Typically this charge is considered if you have passengers in your vehicle. Additionally, in some instances your DUI charge may be amended to Reckless Endangerment. Such an amendment may occur when Reckless Driving is not acceptable due to the required 30 day license suspension. Reckless Endangerment does not have a mandatory driver's license suspension.

The statutory definition for Reckless Endangerment, RCW 9A.36.050, reads as follows:

> A person is guilty of reckless endangerment when he or she recklessly engages in conduct not amounting to drive-by shooting but that creates a substantial risk of death or serious physical injury to another person.

Negligent Driving in the First Degree

RCW 46.61.5249

Negligent Driving in the First Degree is a Misdemeanor and has a maximum penalty of 90 days in jail and a $1,000.00 fine. Additionally, like Reckless Driving, there are no mandatory penalties with this charge and subsequent conviction. There is no driver license suspension, no mandatory jail, and no mandatory requirement to carry SR-22 high risk insurance.

It is important to remember that unlike a DUI you do not need to be impaired to be convicted of Negligent Driving in the First Degree. Technically, if you have a sip of beer and drive in a negligent manner you can be arrested for Negligent Driving in the First Degree.

The statutory definition of Negligent Driving in the First

Degree, RCW 46.61.5259, reads as follows:

> A person is guilty of negligent driving in the first degree if he or she operates a motor vehicle in a manner that is both negligent and endangers or is likely to endanger any person or property, and exhibits the effects of having consumed liquor or an illegal drug.

Negligent Driving in the Second Degree

RCW 46.61.525

With the exception of a dismissal, the amendment of a DUI charge to Negligent Driving in the Second Degree is regarded the best possible result possible. Negligent Driving in the Second Degree is not a criminal offense but a civil traffic infraction. Therefore this offense does not result in a criminal conviction and hence there is no jail.

The statutory definition of Negligent Driving in the Second Degree, RCW 46.61.525, reads as follows:

> (1)(a) A person is guilty of negligent driving in the second degree if, under circumstances not constituting negligent driving in the first degree, he or she operates a motor vehicle in a manner that is both negligent and endangers or is likely to endanger any person or property.

Pre-Trial Diversion Agreement

The Pre-Trial Diversion Agreement, also known as a "Stipulated Order of Continuance" is perhaps a dying breed. The agreement is between you and the City or State and in essence puts you on "probation" for a set period of time with certain conditions, such as lawful behavior, an alcohol/drug evaluation and follow up (treatment or ADIS), DUI Victim's Panel, and a fine. In exchange, at the end of the agreement your case will be either dismissed or amended to a lesser charge. On the other hand, if you do not follow through with the conditions the agreement will be revoked, there will be no trial, and the judge will simply read the police report and almost certainly find you guilty of the charge or charges. There is much at stake but in many instances this type of agreement works well for both those charged with a crime and the jurisdiction.

Unfortunately in Washington State, the Supreme Court has questioned the validity of these agreements. As a result most State courts are now not offering these agreements although there are a few municipal courts that still do.

Penalties

The penalty phase has been addressed elsewhere in the book and the specific penalties for Washington State are at the beginning of this chapter. However, mandatory electronic home monitoring (EHM) for repeat DUI offenders must be re-addressed. Although EHM is mandatory if the defendant has a prior offense within 7 years, under certain conditions EHM may be waived by the Judge.

If you have a prior DUI offense within 7 years (or the DUI was amended to another criminal charge), EHM is mandatory and in addition to actual jail. In cases where EHM is mandatory it may not be waived by the court except under limited circumstances as detailed in RCW 46.61.5055(10):

A court may waive the electronic home monitoring requirements chapter when:

(a) The offender does not have a dwelling, telephone service, or any other necessity to operate an electronic home monitoring system;

(b) The offender does not reside in the state of Washington;

(c) The court determines that there is reason to believe that the offender would violate the conditions of the electronic home monitoring penalty.

Deferred Prosecution

Washington State offers those who have been charged with a DUI a program that is unique to this state. Deferred prosecution permits those who are alcohol or drug dependent or suffer from mental health issues to enter into a two year treatment program in exchange for a complete dismissal of the charge (or charges) in five years, no jail, and no loss of license. RCW 10.05. This program is a godsend for many but the consequences for failure to strictly adhere to the program can be horrendous.

The Washington legislature has recognized that some people who are charged with criminal offenses are not necessarily criminal by nature but suffer from a problem that needs treatment. The legislature has recognized that the best way to keep an alcoholic (or drug addict) from driving drunk (or affected by drugs) is to get him or her to stop drinking or abusing drugs. From this belief came the deferred prosecution statute.

The deferred prosecution statute allows you to petition (ask) the court for a deferral or postponement of their case for a period of five years while you seek treatment for your dependency problem. If the Petition is granted the advantages are obvious: you keep your license, keep the DUI (and/or other charges that were a product of the DUI) off your record, avoid being fined, and, except for cases of where those charged refused the blood or breath test, avoid administrative license suspensions. Importantly, you are given an opportunity to sober up and regain control of your life.

In order to qualify for deferred prosecution, you must obtain an evaluation from a state approved treatment agency. The treatment facility will conduct a detailed assessment and if it concludes that the criminal conduct was the result of alcoholism, drug addiction or mental health problems and that you are amenable to treatment, meaning you are serious about treatment and willing to be treated, you are eligible for deferred prosecution as long as you have never been granted a deferred prosecution before. You are only permitted one per lifetime!

If you are considering entering in the Deferred Prosecution program in Washington it is critical that you and your attorney be familiar with the court where the Petition for Deferred Prosecution will be entered. Every court has its own rules and procedures that you must follow in order to qualify. For example, in Snohomish County District Courts you must submit the Petition for Deferred to the probation department for review more than one week prior to your court date. The paperwork consists of several documents including, but not limited to, the evaluation, a treatment status update, the Petition and Order for Deferred, and a Driving Status Form. Additionally, you must have completed no less than 36 hours of treatment prior to the review of your documents. If any of these documents are not sufficient then the Deferred Prosecution is not approved. In Island County you must meet with a probation officer who reviews the submitted documents and interviews you to ensure that you are a good candidate for the program. Long story short, every court has different procedures and your attorney must know these procedures and advise you of them.

In DUI cases the most frequent reason an individual wishes to enter into the deferred prosecution program is because of a drinking problem. The program consists of a statutorily required two-year treatment program which is broken down to a demanding three phase schedule. The first phase is typically three or four nights a week (sometimes five nights a week depending on the provider) for the first two or three months (seventy -two hours of treatment in the first 90 days) or can involve an inpatient program. Phase two involves weekly treatment and counseling for six months. Phase three, the least rigorous of the three phases, requires counseling once a month for the balance of the two-year program. Additionally, two Alcoholics Anonymous or other self-help meetings per week are required for the full two years. Additionally, you are placed on supervised probation which involves meeting on a regular basis with a probation officer and to pay for those services. The cost can vary, but typically it is approximately $50 per month for the first two years and an annual flat fee for each of the remaining three years. The probation costs vary depending on which jurisdiction you are in, but the numbers quoted are typically what you could expect. Additionally, an ignition interlock device (IID) will be required for at least one year.

If you submitted to a blood or breath test, a deferred prosecution will save your license. This is clearly one of the big benefits to the program. However, in the case of a test refusal, you will still face a license suspension unless you prevail at the DOL hearing.

Three years after the completion of the deferred prosecution treatment program (total of 5 years), the charge(s) is dismissed. What you are required to do during the three years after treatment ends and the case is dismissed, is to stay out of criminal trouble and adhere to all of the requirements imposed by the judge. Typically, the judge will require you to continue with AA attendance and maintain law abiding behavior.

If you are considering doing the deferred prosecution program you should do so seriously. This program is not for the faint of heart and failure will bring dire consequences as the court demands strict compliance. I meet with every client who decides to do the program to ensure that they know exactly what they are getting into. The program can be a great way to deal with a serious legal matter, your ability to drive, and a significant health issue.

It is important that you address important key issues prior to entering into the program to limit the risk of failure. These include:

- Do you need treatment?
- Are you amendable and committed to treatment?
- Do you have the support of family and friends?
- Are you willing to change your lifestyle?
- Will your schedule permit the demands of treatment?
- Can you afford treatment?
- Will your insurance pay for treatment (whole or in part)?
- Do you like the treatment agency?
- Do you like the treatment counselor(s)?

- Is the treatment agency's location convenient for you?

If you fail to comply with the deferred prosecution the results are ominous – the charge of a DUI will result in a conviction and any other accompanying charges will result in convictions. Further, if you fail to comply the penalties that would normally be imposed will possibly be harsher than if you had simply plead guilty originally. Judges look at deferred prosecutions as a privilege and are none too impressed if you fail to fulfill your required duties.

An important point to remember when considering a deferred prosecution is that you are permitted only one per lifetime. Therefore if you are not completely committed to recovery you would be foolish to enter into a deferred prosecution. Additionally, if you are a first time offender you must carefully consider if you want to use your one deferred prosecution allowance for the first time offense or if you want to reserve it just in case you re-offend.

Finally, a deferred prosecution is considered a prior offense if you are subsequently convicted of a DUI within seven years. Therefore, if you are charged (and convicted) of another DUI within seven years the deferred prosecution will be used to substantially enhance the mandatory minimum penalties to be imposed on the subsequent DUI.

If you successfully complete the deferred prosecution you will significantly benefit from the rewards of the program, both legally and personally. Your DUI (and any other charges that were included in the deferred prosecution) will be dismissed and you will have also benefited from the completed treatment and, hopefully, new found sobriety.

As mentioned the deferred prosecution program is statutorily derived. Therefore, although statutes are not particularly exciting to read, in the case of a deferred prosecution they are necessary, hence the inclusion of two of the most important components of the deferred prosecution program, RCW 10.05.020 and RCW 10.05.150.

LICENSES

Ignition Interlock License

In Washington State a specific license called the Ignition Interlock Driver License (IIL) is offered and allows the suspended driver to drive vehicles equipped with an ignition interlock device, so long as the suspension was the result of an alcohol-related DUI or Physical Control. The requirements are that the driver must have been arrested for, or convicted of, an alcohol-related DUI or Physical Control; must have had a valid driver license; must not have been convicted of vehicular assault or vehicular homicide within 7 years before the incident for which you are requesting an IIL; and the current suspension or revocation isn't for, or doesn't include, Minor in Possession, Reckless Driving reduced from an alcohol-related DUI, Vehicular Assault, Vehicular Homicide, or Habitual Traffic Offender.

Importantly, when driving with an IIL, the driver must maintain an interlock device on all vehicles that are driven, including employer's vehicles you drive during work hours. The driver cannot drive a commercial motor vehicle while you have an IIL.

However, this license seems to be useless if you must driver an employer's vehicle while your license is suspended. However, this requirement may be waived if the employer signs an Employer Declaration for Ignition Interlock Waiver.

The application for the IIL requires the Ignition Interlock to be installed and SR 22 insurance obtained. Proof of both must be submitted to the DOL prior to the application being approved. Go to www.washdui.com and click on "driver's license" for details and the application for the IIL.

Occupational/Restricted Driver's License

If the original charge of DUI is amended to Reckless Driving and you receive a license suspension of 30 days, you cannot drive unless you apply for and receive an occupational driver's license. The DOL will grant an occupational license only if you work in an occupation that makes it essential that you drive a motor vehicle. The occupational license does not permit you drive to and from school, transport children to child care, do grocery shopping, or even for medical emergencies. It is very limited and the DOL will specify the hours of the day the license may be used (twelve hours maximum) and may even dictate the routes you may travel. If you fail to follow the conditions mandated by the DOL you will have committed a crime that is punishable by jail, fines and further suspension of your license. Therefore, if granted the privilege do not abuse it.

To apply for the occupational driver's license submit proof of SR 22 insurance and file the application with the Department of Licensing with a $100 application fee. Go to www.washdui.com and click on "important links" for details and the application for the Occupational Driver's License.

Commercial Driver's License (CDL)

As mentioned elsewhere in this book, a charge of DUI may impact your CDL tremendously. Further, even a reduction from DUI to a lesser offense may still potentially harm your CDL. As always, the key is educating yourself regarding the potential dangers that come with a DUI charge and the almost inevitable fallout follows.

Importantly, you may lose your CDL privilege whether you are arrested for DUI while driving a commercial vehicle or a private car. However, it is considered far more severe if you are arrested for DUI while driving a commercial vehicle. Therefore the restrictions and applicable laws are far stricter than regular DUIs.

The demands that you not drive, operate, or be in physical control of a commercial motor vehicle while having alcohol concentration of 0.04 or more. Further, law enforcement shall issue an out-of-service order valid for twenty-four hours against a person who drives, operates, or is in physical control of a commercial motor vehicle while having alcohol in his or her system or who refuses to take a test to determine his or her alcohol content as provided by RCW 46.25.120. RCW 46.25.110

In Washington State a CDL holder has specific duties if he is convicted of a driving related crime. A CDL holder who is convicted of violating a state law or local ordinance relating to motor vehicle traffic control, in any other state or federal, provincial, territorial, or municipal laws of Canada, other than parking violations, shall notify the DOL thirty days of the date of conviction and also his employer in writing of the conviction within thirty days of the conviction. RCW 46.25.030(1)(a)(b) Similarly, a CDL holder must also notify his employer if his driver's license is suspended, revoked, or canceled by a state, who loses the privilege to drive a commercial motor vehicle in a state for any period, or who is disqualified from driving a commercial motor vehicle for any period. RCW 46.25.030(1)(d) Such notification must take place before the end of the business day following the day the driver received notice of that fact.

In the DUI context the CDL holder is disqualified from driving a commercial motor vehicle for a period of not less than one year if he is suspended pursuant to a Department of Licensing ruling or if the person has been convicted of a first violation, of DUI or driving a commercial motor vehicle while the alcohol concentration in the person's system is 0.04 or more, or driving a noncommercial motor vehicle while the alcohol concentration in the person's system is 0.08 or more, or is 0.02 or more if the person is under age twenty-one. RCW 46.25.090

Unfortunately for the CDL holder the disqualification of their license may also occur even if the DUI has been amended. Such examples include the disqualification of the CDL for not less than 60 days if there is a conviction of reckless driving where there has been a prior serious traffic violation or 120 days if convicted of reckless driving where there has been two or more prior serious traffic violations.

Important Washington State Statutes & Case Law

Statutes (RCW & WAC)

Alcohol and Drug Information School (ADIS): RCW 46.61.5056/WAC 388-805

Alcohol Evaluation: RCW 46.61.5056

Alcohol Treatment: RCW 70.96A / RCW 74.50 (ADATSA)

Blood Test Administration: WAC 448-14

Boating Under the Influence (BUI): RCW 79A.60.040

Breath Test Administration: WAC 448-16

Deferred Prosecution: RCW 10.05

Driving Under the Influence (DUI): RCW 46.61.502

DUI Penalties: RCW 46.61.5055

DUI Victim's Panel: RCW 46.61.5152

Electronic Home Monitoring: RCW 9.94A.734

Felony DUI: RCW 46.61.502

Fines: RCW 46.61.5055

Ignition Interlock Device: RCW 46.20.720

Ignition Interlock License: WAC 308-107

Insurance: RCW 46.29

Jail: RCW 46.61.5055

Juvenile DUI (Minor DUI): RCW 46.61.503

Negligent Driving in the First Degree: RCW 46.61.5249

Negligent Driving in the Second Degree: RCW 46.61.525

PBT (Breath Alcohol Screening Test): WAC 448-15

Physical Control: RCW 46.61.504

Reckless Driving: RCW 46.61.500

Reckless Endangerment: RCW 9A.36.050

Rules of the Road: RCW 46.61

State Toxicologist: WAC 448-14

Vehicle Impound: RCW 46.55.113
Work Crew: RCW 9.94A.725
Work Release: RCW 72.65

DUI Case Law
Blood
City of Kent v. Beigh, 145 Wn.2d 33, 32 P.3d 258 (2001)
State v. Curran, 116 Wn.2d 174, 804 P.2d 558 (1991)

Breath Alcohol Ratio – Constitutionality
State v. Brayman, 110 Wn.2d 183, 751 P.2d 294 (1988)

Chemical Tests – Not Necessary to Prove Intoxication
State v. Woolbright, 57 Wn.App. 697, 789 P.2d 815 (1990)

Citizen Informant
Campbell v. Department of Licensing, 31 Wn.App. 833, 644 P.2d 1219 (1982)

Collateral Estoppel
Thompson v. Department of Licensing, 138 Wn.2d 783, 982 P.2d 601 (1999)

Confrontation Right
Lytle v. Department of Licensing, 94 Wn. App. 357, 971 P.2d 969 (1999)

Corpus Delicti
City of Bremeton v. Corbett, 106 Wn.2d 569 (2000)
State v. Flowers, 99 Wn.App. 57, 991 P.2d 1206 (2000)
State v. Sjogren, 71 Wn.App. 779 (1993)

State v. Hamrick, 19 Wn.App. 417, 576 P.2 912 (1978)

Deferred Prosecution
State v. Sell, 110 Wn.App. 741, 43 P.3d 1246 (2002)
City of Walla Walla v. Topel, 104 Wn.App. 816, 17 P.3d 1244 (2001)
City of Kent v. Jenkins, 99 Wn.App. 287, 992 P.2d 1045 (2000)
Alwood v. Harper, 94 Wn.App. 396, 973 P.2d 12 (1999)
State v. Bays, 90 Wn.App. 731, 954 P.2d 301 (1998)
State v. Vinge, 59 Wn.App. 134, 795 P.1199 (1990)
State v. Glasser, 37 Wn.App. 131, 678 P.2d 827 (1984)

Field Sobriety Tests
City of Seattle v. Stalsbroten, 138 Wn.2d 227, 978 P.2d 1059 (1999)
Hienemann v. Whitman, 105 Wn.2d 796, 718 P.2d 789 (1986)

Horizontal Gaze Nystagmus
Frye v. United States, 293 F.1013, 34 A.L.R. 145 (1923)
State v. Baity, 140 Wn.2d 1, 991 P.2d 1151 (2000)
State v. Koch, 126 Wn.App. 589 (2005)
State v. Cissne, 72 Wn.App. 677, 685 P.2d 564 (1994)

Implied Consent Warnings
Department of Licensing v. Grewal, 108 Wn. App. 815, 33 P.3d 94 (2001)
State v. Bostrom, 127 Wn.2d 580, 902 P.2d 157 (1995)
State v. Staeheli, 102 Wn.2d 305, 685 P.2d 591 (1984)

Interrogation
State v. Johnson, 48 Wn. App. 681, 739 P.2d 1209 (1987)

Language – Interpreters
State v. Prok, 107 Wn.2d 153, 727 P.2d 652 (1986)

Negligent Driving 1ˢᵗ Degree
City of Walla Walla v. Greene, 154 Wn.2d 722 (2005)

Operating a Vehicle
City of Sunnyside v. Wendt, 51 Wn.App. 846, 755 P.2d 847 (1988)

Physical Control
State v. Beck, 42 Wn.App. 12, 707 P.2d 1380 (1985)
State v. Smelter, 36 Wn.App. 439, 674 P.2d 690 (1984)
McGuire v. City of Seattle, 31 Wn.App. 438, 642 P.2d 765 (1982)

Physical Control – Safely off the Roadway
State v. Hazzard, 43 Wn.App. 335, 716 P.2d 977 (1986)

Prescription Drugs – Defense to DUI
Kaiser v. Suburban Transp. Sys., 65 Wn.2d 461, 398 P.2d 14 (1965)

Pretext Stops
State v. Ladson, 138 Wn.2d 343, 979 P.2d 833 (1999)

Pretrial Conditions (reasonable)
Butler v. Kato, 137 Wn. App. 515, 524 154 P.3d 259 (2007)

Probable Cause
State v. Gillenwater, 96 Wn. App. 667, 980 P.2d 318 (1999)
Bokor v. Department of Licensing, 74 Wn. App. 523, 874 P.2d 168 (1994)
O'Neill v. Department of Licensing, 62 Wn. App. 112, 813 P.2d 166 (1991)
State v. Kennedy, 107 Wn.2d 1, 726 P.2d 445 (1986)
State v. Terrovona, 105 Wn.2d 632, 716 P.2d 295 (1986)

Right to Counsel
State v. Trevino, 127 Wn.2d 735, 903 P.2d 447 (1995)

Roadway – Definition includes Parking Lot
City of Edmonds v. Ostby, 48 Wn.App. 867, 740 P.2d 916 (1987)

Reckless Driving
City of Redmond v. Bagby, 155 Wn.2d 59 (2005)

Refusal
Rockwell v. Department of Licensing, 94 Wn. App. 531, 972 P.2d 1276 (1999)
Department of Licensing v. Lax, 125 Wn.2d 818, 888 P.2d 1190 (1995)
State v. Long, 113 Wn.2d 266, 778 P.2d 1027 (1989)

Safely Off the Road
State v. Votava, 149 Wn.2d 178, 66 P.3d 1050 (2003)

Sentencing
Walla Walla v. Greene, Docket Number 75108-1 (2005)

Statements
Crawford v. Washington, 541 U.S. 36 (2004)

Two-Hour Rule
State v. Crediford, 130 Wn.2d 747, 927 P.2d 1129 (1996)

Under the Influence – Definition
State v. Hurd, 5 Wn.2d 308, 105 P.2d 59 (1940)

CHAPTER **14**

Definitions

-A-

Absorption (of alcohol in the body) – This is the process by which alcohol enters the blood circulation after ingestion.

Acquittal - A finding by a judge or jury that a person who was tried for committing a crime is not guilty.

ADIS (Alcohol/Drug Information School) - Is an 8-hour program designed to educate the participants about the dangers of alcohol and drugs.

Administrative License Suspension - This relates to penalties imposed by the Department of Licensing and is a law that allows the prompt suspension of the license of drivers charged with a DUI when a driver has a BAC above the prescribed limit, or if the driver refuses to take a blood or breath test. These sanctions are separate from district or municipal court penalties.

Affidavit - A written statement of fact that is verified by oath or affirmation before a notary public. These are commonly introduced into court proceedings to verify some fact or to confirm that some act has been accomplished.

Affidavit of prejudice - A written motion by a party to a judge requesting that the judge not hear the case.

Affirmative Defense - Without denying the charge, the defendant raises extenuating or mitigating circumstances to avoid criminal responsibility. The defendant usually must prove (or set forth some evidence of) any affirmative defense he/she raises. Court rules or state statutes typically require a defendant to notify the opponent before the trial that an affirmative defense will be asserted.

Alcohol - Derived from Arabic. Refers to a wide range of chemicals, whether suited for human consumption or not. The term "alcohol" is often used by lay persons to refer to alcoholic beverages. The usual type of alcohol found in mixed drinks, wine and beer is ethanol.

Alcohol Dependence - The need for repeated doses of alcohol in order to feel good or to avoid feeling bad. In its unqualified form, dependence refers to both physical and psychological elements. Psychological or psychic dependence refers to the experience of impaired control over drinking, and physiological or physical dependence refers to tolerance and withdrawal symptoms. In biologically-oriented discussion, dependence is often used to refer only to physical dependence.

Alcohol Evaluation - An assessment conducted by a state-certified drug and alcohol treatment agency to evaluate the defendant's alcohol usage patterns, potential problems, and recommended treatment.

Evaluation takes approximately one hour. Treatment may require one, eight hour class or up to a two years ongoing treatment.

Alford Plea - The so-called *Alford* plea is a form of "guilty" plea in which the defendant does not admit the act, but admits that sufficient evidence exists with which the prosecution could likely convince a judge or jury to find the defendant guilty. Upon receiving an *Alford* plea from a defendant, the court may immediately pronounce the defendant guilty and impose sentence as if the defendant had otherwise been convicted of the crime. This plea originated in the United States Supreme Court case of *North Carolina v. Alford*, 400 U.S. 25 (1970).

Alibi - A "lack of presence" defense. Defendant need not prove that he was elsewhere when the crime happened; rather, a Prosecutor must *dis*prove a claimed alibi (i.e., Prosecutor must prove beyond a reasonable doubt that the defendant was present). Although rare in DUI cases, some drivers may not be present after an accident when the police arrive at the scene.

Alleged (allegation) - Stated; recited; claimed; asserted; charged.

Appeal - Review of a case by a higher court.

Appearance - The formal proceeding by which a defendant submits to the jurisdiction of the court.

Arraignment - First court appearance after being arrested. The defendant appears before a judge to hear the charges brought against him/her, set bail if necessary, and conditions of release. The defendant enters a plea of not guilty or guilty.

Attorney at law - A lawyer who is licensed to act as a representative for another in a legal matter or proceeding.

Attorney of record - An attorney, named in the records of a case, who is responsible for handling the case on behalf of the party he or she represents.

Attorney-Client Agreement - This is a written contract between the attorney and client. This outlines what the amount owing to the attorney is, including the amount of the retainer and what the monthly payments are, if any, the obligations the attorney may have to you and you to the attorney, and any information regarding any payment defaults.

Attorney-Client Privilege - In all legal matters, the client (whether or not a party to litigation) has a privilege to refuse to disclose, and to prevent another from disclosing, a confidential communication between client and lawyer. The attorney-client privilege authorizes a client to refuse to disclose, and to prevent others from disclosing, information communicated in confidence to the attorney and legal advice received in return. The objective of the privilege is to enhance the value which society places upon legal representation by assuring the client the opportunity for full disclosure to the attorney, unfettered by fear that others will be informed. While the privilege belongs only to the client, the attorney is professionally obligated to claim it on his client's behalf whenever the opportunity arises unless he has been instructed otherwise by the client.

-B-

BAC - Short for "blood alcohol concentration." BAC refers to the amount of alcohol in your bloodstream and is measured in percentages. BAC can be measured either by breath, blood or urine testing and is often used by law enforcement to determine whether or not a motorist is "legally drunk."

BAC DataMaster and DataMaster CDM - Machines that measures BAC according to the amount of alcohol concentration on the breath. Utilized in many States.

BAC Refusal - Refusal to blow into the breath machine at the police station or take a blood test as requested by police officers.

Bail - To set free a person arrested or imprisoned (pending trial or resolution of an appeal), in exchange for security such as cash, credit card deposit or real estate. Bail is forfeited if the person fails to appear in court as directed.

Bail bond - An agreement by a third party to pay a certain sum of money if the defendant fails to appear in court.

Bailiff - A court employee who, among other things, maintains order in the courtroom and is responsible for custody of the jury.

Bench Warrant - A warrant that is issued by a judge for the arrest of a person who fails to appear for a court appearance.

Beyond a Reasonable Doubt – The highest level of proof in any legal matters, reserved for criminal cases. In order for a criminal defendant to be convicted of a crime, the prosecutor must prove his or her case to the point that the jurors have no reasonable doubts in their minds that the defendant did whatever he or she is charged with having done. The typical jury in criminal cases must be unanimous, but some jurisdictions now allow verdicts on less than unanimous verdicts for juries with more than 6 members.

Blood-breath partition ratio - Presumed ratio between concentration of alcohol in alveolar (deep lung) air and the blood: approximately 2100:1 (aka "Blood-breath presumption"), which if not in fact as presumed may cause breath test error.

Bond - In criminal law, a surety bond assures the appearance of the defendant or the payment of the defendant's bail if the defendant fails to appear. The person who agrees to be the "surety" is financially obligated to pay the bond if the person fails to appear. The failure to appear will typically cause the judge of the court requiring attendance to issue a "bond forfeiture" order, as well as a warrant for the defendant's arrest.

Blood Test - A test to measure a person's BAC by drawing the blood, usually done in a hospital or at the jail. Blood tests are often requested where substances other than alcohol are suspected to be impairing the driver in a DUI case, or where an accident may require that the person suspected of drunk driving is already going to a hospital. In some states, refusal is possible for a person who is capable of refusing. In other states, forcible blood draws are authorized.

Breath Test - A test to measure your breath alcohol content, usually done at a police station or a jail. One does not have to agree to blow into a breath machine, and in most cases should not agree to do so. Some police jurisdictions also use roadside breath tests, but these are not usually admissible as evidence in court.

Brief - A legal document, prepared by an attorney, which presents the law and facts supporting his or her client's case.

BUI - Boating Under the Influence.

Burden of Proof - The obligation of a party to prove his allegations during a trial. Different levels of proof are required depending on the type of case. This phrase is employed to signify the duty of proving the facts in dispute on an issue raised between the parties in a cause. In criminal cases, as every person is presumed to be innocent until the contrary is proved, the burden of proof rests on the prosecutor to prove each and every element of the charges. After the prosecutor has presented such evidence, the defendant may need to rebut (challenge) the prosecutor's evidence, as a practical matter, even though the burden of proof in criminal cases never shifts to the defendant.

-C-

Calendar - List of cases arranged for hearing in court.

Calibration - A process of adjusting a measuring device to a standard so as to ascertain the correction factors required for accurate measurement.

Case - Any proceeding, action, cause, lawsuit or controversy initiated through the court system by filing a complaint, petition, indictment or information.

Challenge for cause - A request by a party that the court excuse a specific juror on the basis that the juror is biased.

Chambers - A judge's private office.

Charge - Formal accusation of having committed a criminal offense.

Chemical Test - As it relates to DUI, a test of the alcohol or drug concentration in a person's blood. A breath or blood test can be used as chemical tests for alcohol. If other drugs are suspected, a blood test or urine test is used.

Circumstantial evidence - All evidence of indirect nature; the process of decision by which judge or jury may reason from circumstances known or proved to establish by inference the principal fact.

Clerk of court - An officer of a court whose principal duty is to maintain court records and preserve evidence presented during a trial.

Closing argument - The closing statement, by counsel, to the trier of facts after all parties have concluded their presentation of evidence.

Commercial Vehicle - A vehicle driven for business purposes. In the DUI context, there are serious consequences for driving a commercial vehicle while under the influence.

Community Service - Depending on the offense, your state may offer community service as a way to work off fines. Community service may also be a mandatory part of your sentencing.

Complaint - Formal written charge that a person has committed a criminal offense.

Concurrent Sentence - Upon conviction for multiple crimes, a criminal sentence can be ordered by the judge to be served at the same time as another criminal sentence, rather than one after the other.

Conditional License - A conditional license is a license granted "on condition" of something, such as completing a DUI course or alcohol treatment program.

Once that "condition" has been met, a standard license is generally issued or reinstated.

Consecutive Sentence - Upon conviction for multiple crimes, criminal sentences that must be served one after the other, rather than at the same time, are called "consecutive" sentences. Consecutive sentences may only be imposed if there is specific statutory authority to do so. In some circumstances, consecutive sentences may be imposed within the judge's discretion (e.g., when a person is convicted of a new offense committed while on parole status). In other circumstances, consecutive sentences are mandatory under state law.

Contempt of court - Any act that is meant to embarrass, hinder or obstruct a court in the administration of justice. Direct contempt is committed in the presence of the court; indirect contempt is when a lawful order is not carried out or is refused.

Continuance - Postponing or rescheduling a case or court session until another date or time. In some jurisdictions, this is called an "adjournment". Each state's laws control when and under what circumstances an adjournment or continuance is available to either party.

Conviction - Finding that a person is guilty beyond a reasonable doubt of committing a crime.

Corpus delicti - The body or material substance upon which crime has been committed; e.g., the driver of a vehicle in a DUI case.

Corroborating evidence - Evidence supplementary to that already given and tending to strengthen or confirm it.

Court-Appointment Attorney - Refers to legal counsel assigned by the court to represent an indigent criminal defendant. A court-appointed attorney is not necessarily a "free" attorney; the court can order that some or all of the attorney's time utilized on behalf the client be reimbursed.

Court of appeals - Intermediate appellate court to which most appeals are taken from superior court.

Court, district - Court of limited jurisdiction where civil cases up to $50,000 and small claims cases up to $2,500 can be heard. Criminal and gross misdemeanors and traffic citations are also heard in district court.

Court, municipal - Court whose jurisdiction is confined to a city or local community. In Washington, jurisdiction is generally limited to criminal and traffic offenses arising from violation of local ordinances.

Crime - Conduct declared unlawful by a legislative body and for which there is a punishment of a jail or prison term, a fine, or both.

Cross-examination - The questioning of a witness by the party opposed to the one who produced the witness.

Custody - Detaining of a person by lawful process or authority to assure that individual's appearance to any hearing; the jailing or imprisonment of a person convicted of a crime.

-D-

Defendant - Person accused of a crime.

Deferred Prosecution - Prosecution of the case is deferred for five years during which time the defendant receives intensive drug or alcohol treatment in a state-certified treatment program. Case is dismissed at the end of five years if program is successfully completed. Only one deferred prosecution is allowed in a lifetime. It also counts as a prior offense if subsequently charged with DUI.

Direct examination - The questioning of a witness by the party who produced the witness.

Discovery – A pretrial proceeding where a party to an action may be informed about (or "discover") the facts known by other parties or witnesses.

Dismissal with prejudice - Dismissal of a case by a judge which bars the losing party from raising the issue again in another lawsuit.

Dismissal without prejudice - The losing party is permitted to sue again with the same cause of action.

District Attorney - A lawyer elected or appointed to serve as a prosecutor for the state in criminal cases.

Docket - A list or index of cases and case events maintained by the clerk of court. This term can also mean a list of cases on a court calendar for a specific day or term of court.

Double jeopardy - Prohibition against more than one prosecution for the same crime.

DRE - Twelve-step Drug Recognition Examination. Field sobriety testing, including measurement of jerking eye movements. *See*"HGN."

DUI - Driving While Under the Influence.

DUI Victim's Panel – See Victim's Panel.

DWI - Driving While Intoxicated.

-E-

Electronic Home Monitoring (EHM) - An alternative to jail time where by the defendant serves his/her jail time at home. This is monitored electronically usually through an ankle bracelet.

Elimination (of alcohol in the body) - Elimination is the removal of alcohol from the body.

Entrapment - The act of officers or agents of a government in inducing a person to commit a crime not contemplated by the person, for the purpose of instituting a criminal prosecution against him or her.

Ethyl Alcohol – This alcohol property is a clear, colorless flammable liquid with a burning taste.

Entrapment - Entrapment occurs when police engage in impermissible conduct that would induce an otherwise law-abiding person to commit a crime in similar circumstances, or when police engage in conduct so reprehensible that it cannot be tolerated by the court. Entrapment does not occur if the defendant has the propensity to commit the crime, and the police conduct only gives the defendant the opportunity to commit the crime. This defense is almost never viable in a DUI case.

Evidence - Any form of proof legally presented at a trial through witnesses, records, documents, etc.

Expert evidence - Testimony given by those qualified to speak with authority regarding scientific, technical or professional matters.

Expungement - A process where a conviction may be set aside either upon the passage of time or the completion of certain conditions. Not available in some states.

Extradition - The formal process of delivering a person found in one state to authorities in another state where that person has been accused or convicted of a crime.

-F-

Felony DUI - A serious crime, such as murder, rape or burglary, for which there is a stricter sentence given than for a misdemeanor. In Washington a DUI will be considered a felony if you had 5 "priors" in the past 10 years.

FST – "Field Sobriety Test." The NHTSA only endorses only three FSTs as sufficiently reliable: a) walk and turn, b) one leg stand and c) HGN tests; but other tests are routinely admitted to convict motorists, including the alphabet test, finger count, etc.

FTA - (acronym for "failure to appear") When a person is issued a traffic citation, accusation, information or complaint and then does NOT show up for court on the stated date and time, the judge will usually order any bond to be forfeited to the court system.

-G-

Gross Misdemeanor: Class of crime where if convicted, sentence can be no more than one year and fine no more than $5000. All DUIs are gross misdemeanors (unless they are felonies).

-H-

Hearsay - A statement made outside of court (i.e., not from the witness stand at the present proceeding) that is offered into evidence not merely to prove that the statement was made but to prove that it was *true*. There are dozens of long-established exceptions to the general rule that hearsay statements are inadmissible in court; the exceptions are based on circumstances where the out-of-court statements carry a likelihood of trustworthiness (e.g., deathbed statements, self-incriminating statements, statements made to doctors about medical conditions, etc.).

High BAC - Threshold blood alcohol content for which maximum penalties and fines may apply, even on a first offense.

Horizontal Gaze Nystagmus (HGN) - A NHTSA approved standardized field sobriety test. "Nystagmus" means an involuntary jerking of the eyes and HGN refers to an involuntary jerking occurring as the eyes gaze toward the side. Involuntary jerking of the eyes becomes readily noticeable when a person is impaired. As a person's blood alcohol concentration increases, the eyes begin to jerk sooner as they move to the side. When performed properly and in a controlled environment is the most reliable FST. See also Vertical Gaze Nystagmus.

Hung jury - A jury whose members cannot agree on a verdict.

-I-

Ignition Interlock Device (IID) - An ignition interlock device is an in-car alcohol breath screening device that prevents a vehicle from starting if it detects a blood alcohol concentration (BAC) over a pre-set limit (i.e. 0.02 or as mandated by the court). The device is located inside the vehicle, near the driver's seat, and is connected to the engine's ignition system. Many states require that the device be used by those convicted of DUI, and in Washington it is mandatory for at least one year if convicted of a DUI.

Ignition Interlock License (IIL) – An ignition interlock license permits a driver to drive even though his license was suspended due to a DUI or Physical Control arrest or conviction.

Impeachment of a witness - An attack on the credibility of a witness by the testimony of other witnesses.

Inadmissible - That which, under the established rules of evidence, cannot be admitted or received.

Implied Consent Laws - Some states have implied consent laws, including Washington State. If you have a driver's license in one of these states, you have, by implication, consented to being pulled over by a police officer to have your blood alcohol concentration measured. In many states, you may refuse to take the test, but fines and license suspensions may be the result.

Infrared Spectroscopy - A technique for determining the identity of a substance and the quantity of the substance by exposing the substance to infrared energy and analyzing the nature and amount of absorption by the substance.

Interferant - A chemical substance other than the substance of interest that may create a false positive or elevated reading.

-J-

Judge - An elected or appointed public official with authority to hear and decide cases in a court of law.

Judge, pro tem - Temporary judge.

Judgment - Final determination by a court of the rights and claims of the parties in an action.

Jurisdiction - The right and power to interpret and apply the law to a particular case. One definition relates to the authority of a court to hear and rule upon certain types of cases. This is sometimes called "subject matter jurisdiction". This term can also refer to a limitation on the extent of authority or control. By way of example, the law in some states limits the place or geographic area that a police officer can arrest a person to being the area where a crime is committed and observed within the officer's "jurisdiction" (e.g., the City Limits).

Jury - A number of people, selected according to law, and sworn to listen to certain matters of fact and declare the truth upon evidence presented to them. In a criminal case, panels of 6 or 12 jurors (depending on state law) can hear misdemeanor offense cases, and 12 will typically be required to hear felony cases.

Jury Selection – see "Voir Dire"

-L-

License Revocation/Suspension - Administrative sanction whereby drivers' license is taken away. To get license back, defendant must show proof of SR22 insurance (high-risk insurance), ignition interlock installation (if required), and pay a reissue fee.

-M-

Misdemeanor - Offenses considered less serious than felonies. There are two classes of misdemeanors—simple and gross. A simple misdemeanor has maximum penalties of $1,000 fine and 90 days in jail. A gross misdemeanor has maximum penalties of $5,000 fine and 365 days in jail.

Miranda Warnings - A warning given by police before custodial interrogation. It advises the person that he does not have to talk to police, and that his silence will not be held against him, and his right to legal counsel before talking to police. This "phrase" derives from a US Supreme Court decision: *Miranda v Arizona*, 384 US 436 (1966). Over the years, courts at every level have curved dozens of exceptions into the rule so that its effect is watered down.

Mistrial - Erroneous or invalid trial. Usually declared because of prejudicial error in the proceedings or when there was a hung jury.

Motion Hearing - A hearing before the trial where legal issues are disputed. Typically, the defense will try to keep out evidence such as BAC DataMaster test, field sobriety tests or defendant's statements.

Motion in Limine - (Latin: "at the threshold") is a motion made before the start of a trial requesting that the judge rule that certain evidence may, or may not, be introduced to the jury in a trial.

-O-

Objection - Statement by an attorney taking exception to testimony or the attempted admission of evidence and opposing its consideration as evidence.

Omnibus hearing - A pretrial hearing normally scheduled at the same time the trial date is established. Purpose of the hearing is to ensure each party receives (or "discovers") vital information concerning the case held by the other. In addition, the judge may rule on the scope of discovery or on the admissibility of challenged evidence.

Opening statement - The initial statement made by attorneys for each side, outlining the facts each intends to establish during the trial.

Open Container Laws - In some states, it is illegal to have an open container of alcohol in your vehicle. Many states have laws that make it illegal for drivers and passengers to have open containers in the vehicle.

-P-

Per Se – Latin. "Of, in, or by itself or oneself; intrinsically." In DUI practice, all the prosecutor needs to prove to obtain a conviction for this type of "DUI" offense is to successfully introduce the breath or blood test result to convince the jury or judge that the result obtained was reliable and trustworthy, as required under state law.

Peremptory challenge - Procedure which parties in an action may use to reject prospective jurors without giving a reason. Each side is allowed a limited number of such challenges.

Perjury - Making intentionally false statements under oath. Perjury is a criminal offense.

Personal recognizance - In criminal proceedings, the pretrial release of a defendant without bail upon the defendant's promise to return to court.

Plea – A criminal defendant's official statement of "guilty" or "not guilty" to the charge.

Plea Bargain – This term generally refers to an agreement in a criminal case in which a prosecutor and a defense lawyer (acting on his/her client's behalf) arrange to settle the case against the defendant on some negotiated terms and conditions. Plea bargaining is an essential part of the criminal justice machine in the United States. Indeed, an overwhelming majority of criminal cases in the United States are settled by way of plea bargains rather than by seeking trial before a judge or jury. Generally, a plea bargain allows the prosecution and defense to agree on the outcome and resolve the pending charge without a trial. In colloquial terms this is known as "copping a plea".

Physical Control – very similar to a DUI but the individual does not actually drive a motor vehicle but is found to be in "physical control" of the vehicle while under the influence of alcohol (or with a BAC at or over 0.08).

Precedent - Previously decided case which is recognized as an authority for determining future cases.

Preliminary Breath Test Machine (PBT) - Designed to measure BAC in exhaled breath. These units are used at the scene of the DUI and are not admissible at trial and are used to help determine probable cause to arrest only.

Presumption of Innocence - The Government has the burden of proving a person charged with a crime guilty beyond a reasonable doubt, and if it fails to do so the person is (so far as the law is concerned) not guilty. The indictment or formal charge against any person is not evidence of guilt. Indeed, the person is presumed by the law to be innocent. The law does not require a person to prove his innocence or produce any evidence at all.

Pretrial Diversion - Also known as a "stipulated order of continuance" (SOC). A program in which a defendant is essentially put on "probation" for a set period of time and his or her case does not go to trial during that time. If the defendant meets the conditions set by the court, then the charge will either be dismissed or amended to a less serious charge. These "civil agreements" were once widely used but in Washington State a recent Washington State finding has put these tools in danger of extinction.

Pretrial Hearing - A hearing after arraignment and before the trial. The attorneys tell the court what motions they will be bringing and often negotiate plea bargains at this time. The case is either set for trial, a plea is entered, or a continuance is granted. Often there is more than one pretrial hearing.

Pro Se - Latin for "on one's own behalf" A person who represents himself in court alone without the help of a lawyer is said to appear *pro se.*

Probable Cause - A constitutionally prescribed standard of proof; a reasonable ground for belief in the existence of certain facts. The burden of proof necessary for issuance of an indictment or issuance of a trial information (accusation).

Probation - The release into the community of a defendant who has been found guilty or plead guilty of a crime, typically under certain conditions, such as paying a fine, doing community service, jail, obtaining an alcohol/drug evaluation and any follow up that is required.

Probation Revocation - When a judge has permitted an accused person who either pleads guilty or is found guilty at trial to not go to trial for some portion of the sentence handed down, the judge sets conditions under which the person can stay out of incarceration. The failure of the probationer to follow the judge's "conditions" can and usually does lead to a "probation revocation". Typically, the person is seized (arrested) first. Thereafter, on a fixed schedule of that judge, the violator is given a day in court to explain or challenge the "violation". Individuals who are on probation no longer enjoy all the constitutional protections that he or she had before the guilty (or *nolo contendere*) plea or guilty verdict at trial was rendered. For example, the 'standard of proof' in a criminal trial is the highest in the world: proof beyond a reasonable doubt. In a probation revocation, depending on the state you are facing a revocation in, it is either preponderance of the evidence or probable cause to believe that a violation has occurred. Very little evidence is needed to prove this.

Prosecutor - The public officer in each county who is a lawyer and who represents the interests of the state in criminal trials and the county in all legal matters involving the county. In criminal cases, the prosecutor has the responsibility of deciding who and when to prosecute. Also known as prosecuting attorney.

Provisional (or Restricted) License - A provisional license typically withholds certain license privileges. In a DUI context, a provisional license might be granted to someone to drive to and from work only.

Public Defender - A lawyer employed by the government to represent a person accused of a crime and who cannot afford to hire a lawyer.

-R-

Readiness Hearing - After the pretrial and before the trial. Attorneys tell the court that they are ready for trial and set the trial date. Often additional negotiations are done at the readiness hearing.

Restitution - A legal remedy sometimes allowed by statute under which a person is restored to his or her original position prior to loss or injury. In DUI accident cases, the laws of many jurisdictions authorize the criminal court disposing of a guilty verdict or plea to order restitution of damages to the "victim" of the DUI-related crash.

Retainer - A contract between an attorney and his or her client. The payment of money to the attorney as a "retainer" signifies an agreement for the attorney to act on the person's behalf and to represent the person in the legal matter that is the subject of their "contract."

In criminal cases, a retainer is typically a partial payment toward the ultimate, total fee that may be due in
the event the case requires filing of a variety of motions and other pleadings, handling administrative
license issues, conduction of pre-trial hearings of various types, going to trial or possibly filing an appeal.
To avoid confusion on the exact terms and schedule
of other payments, retainer agreements should be in
writing in virtually all cases.

Retrograde extrapolation - Technique of estimating
the rate at which alcohol ingested is absorbed and
eliminated.

RCW – Revised Code of Washington.

-S-

Search and seizure, unreasonable - In general, an examination without authority of law, of one's premises or
person for the purpose of discovering stolen or illegal
property or some other evidence of guilt to be used in
prosecuting a crime.

Search warrant - A written order, issued by a judge or
magistrate in the name of the state, directing an officer
to search a specified house or other place for stolen
property, drugs, or contraband. Usually required as a
condition for a legal search and seizure.

Sentence - Judgment formally pronounced by a judge
upon defendant after the defendant's conviction in the
criminal prosecution.

Simulator solution - A bottle of heated and agitated solution of alcohol and water with a known solution of
0.08 % alcohol to water. Vapor is measured after mo-

torist breath test to verify if Breathalyzer is operating properly.

Sobriety Checkpoints - A system where law enforcement agencies select a particular location for a particular time period and systematically stop vehicles (for example, every third car) to investigate drivers for possible DUI. If any evidence of intoxication is noted, a detailed investigation ensues. Unconstitutional in many states including Washington.

Speedy Trial – Both federal constitutional law and state constitutional (or statutory) laws may provide a person facing criminal charges with the right to a speedy trial. This defense attack can be raised when the prosecution has waited too long to proceed to trial. Each state controls its own statutes and constitutional protections as to when and under what circumstances the issue can be raised by the defense. Speedy trial challenges may be pursued in cases in which a significant lapse of time has occurred between the date of the alleged commission of the crime and the date of arrest. Also, several states have built-in "presumptive" time limits on various types of cases wherein the prosecution loses if the trial is not completed within a fixed amount of time. Others call for the defense to file a notice of an accused person's desire to resolve the case in accordance with the available statutory or constitutional provisions available to accelerate the trial date. All such statutes and state constitutional provisions authorizing speedy trials contain various exceptions to this rule. For example, if the defense acts to cause a delay (e.g., by requesting an adjournment or continuance), this can cause a "waiver" of this right.

Statute - A law adopted by the legislature.

Statute of limitations - Law which specifies the time within which parties must take judicial action to enforce their rights.

Subpoena - Document issued by the authority of the court to compel a witness to appear and give testimony or produce documentary evidence in a proceeding. Failure to appear or produce is punishable by contempt of court.

Subpoena duces tecum - "Bring the document with you." A process by which the court commands a witness to produce specific documents or records in a trial.

Summons - Document or writ directing the sheriff or other officer to notify a person that an action has been commenced against him or her in court and that he or she is required to appear, on a certain day, and answer the complaint in such action.

-T-

Testimony - Any statement made by a witness under oath in a legal proceeding.

Trial - The presentation of evidence in court to a trier of fact who applies the applicable law to those facts and then decides the case.

Trier of fact - The jury or, in a non-jury trial, the judge.

Two-Hour Rule - Statute provides for admissibility of chemical test consented to by motorist within 2 hours of arrest.

-V-

Vehicle Impound/Immobilization - Vehicle impound is an option used by some states when there has been more than one DUI conviction. The vehicle may be seized, or an ignition interlock device may be installed on the steering wheel of the car, requiring the driver to pass a breath test using the device before he or she can start the vehicle and drive away.

Venue - The specific county, city or geographical area in which a court has jurisdiction. See change of venue.

Verdict - The formal decision or finding made by a jury and accepted by the court.

Vertical Gaze Nystagmus (VGN) – Is an up and down jerking of the eyes which occurs when the eyes gaze upward at maximum elevation. NHTSA claims that the presence of VGN has proven to be a reliable indicator of high doses of alcohol for an individual or certain other drugs.

Victim's Panel - Two hour class taught by DUI victims to relate their experience to people who have been charged or convicted of a DUI or alcohol related offense.

Voir Dire - French for " to speak truly, to tell the truth." An inquiry of prospective jurors by the attorneys (in most jurisdictions) and by the judge, to determine if prospective jurors are qualified for jury duty in a given case. Also called "jury selection."

-W-

WAC – Washington Administrative Code.

Widmark's Formula - In 1932 the Swedish scientist Eric P Widmark developed two formulae commonly used for the calculation of the amount of alcohol ingested and for assessing the concentration of alcohol at some time prior to the sampling. Thought by many to be unreliable and inaccurate.

Witness - Person who testifies under oath before a court, regarding what he or she has seen, heard or otherwise observed.

Work Release - A probation program (alternative to jail sentence) in some jurisdictions wherein the defendant is permitted to maintain employment while residing in jail when not at work. The defendant leaves jail on workdays only for his work hours, plus limited travel time. These programs are not available in some jurisdictions, due to lack of funding for such facilities. Also, some state statutes do not allow DUI detainees to utilize "work release."

-Z-

Zero Tolerance BAC - Allowable blood alcohol content for minors (as defined by the state). This percentage can be as low as 0% (meaning no alcohol content may be detected-hence the term "zero tolerance.") or as high as 0.02%.

ALSO BY David N. Jolly

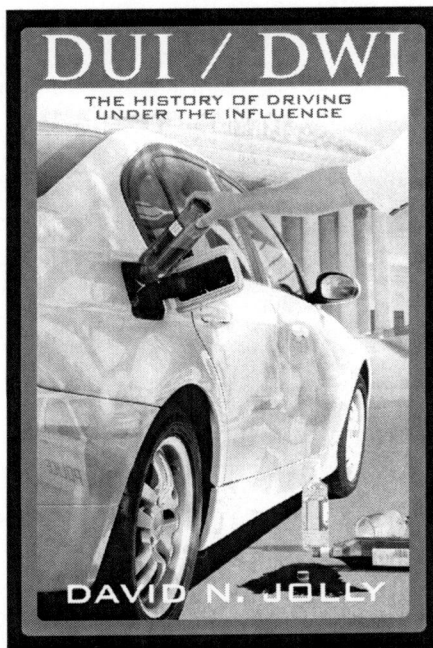

DUI / DWI

The first driving under the influence (DUI) law in the United States was enacted 100 years ago (1910) in New York State. Since this date the law has evolved and the manner in which DUI detection is conducted has been extensively studied and debated. This book provides an objective review of the history of DUI laws, alcohol, drugs, law enforcement, DUI investigations, BAC testing, alcohol/drug evaluations and treatment, DUI organizations, DUI prevention and reoccurrence programs and the future of DUI. This book is the ideal supplement for law enforcement, Judges, prosecuting attorneys, defense attorneys, and anyone involved or interested in the law and prevention of driving under the influence.

Learn more at:
www.outskirtspress.com/historyofdui

CPSIA information can be obtained at www.ICGtesting.com
Printed in the USA
BVOW07s0852280813

329763BV00001B/280/P